Urban Social Movements

SOCIOLOGY, POLITICS AND CITIES

Editor: JAMES SIMMIE

PUBLISHED
Manuel Castells: CITY, CLASS AND POWER
Patrick Dunleavy: URBAN POLITICAL ANALYSIS
Brian Elliott and David McCrone: THE CITY
Roger Friedland: POWER AND CRISIS IN THE CITY
Wyn Grant (ed.): THE POLITICAL ECONOMY OF CORPORATISM
Stuart Lowe: URBAN SOCIAL MOVEMENTS
James Simmie: POWER, PROPERTY AND CORPORATISM

FORTHCOMING
T. R. Gurr and D. S. King: THE STATE AND THE CITY

Urban Social Movements

The City After Castells

STUART LOWE

MACMILLAN

First published 1986

Published by MACMILLAN EDUCATION LTD
Houndmills, Basingstoke, Hampshire RG21 2XS
and London
Companies and representatives
throughout the world

Filmsetting by Vantage Photosetting Co. Ltd
Eastleigh and London

Printed in Hong Kong

British Library Cataloguing in Publication Data
Lowe, Stuart
Urban social movements.— (Sociology, politics
& cities).
1. Social movements   2. Cities and towns
I. Title   II. Series
303.4′84   HM131
ISBN 0–333–37519–X
ISBN 0–333–37520–3 Pbk

For Sue

Contents

General Editor's Preface

SOCIOLOGY, POLITICS AND CITIES

Cities are the focal points of economic, political and cultural life in most countries. They are the places where the results of past and present economic and political conflicts leave their most obvious marks. To understand the changing characteristics of cities, it is therefore necessary to comprehend the relationships between economic and political forces and the influence they have on the lives of different citizens.

The series 'Sociology, Politics and Cities' provides a vehicle for the exploration of these relationships. As they cannot be understood within the confines of traditional single disciplinary boundaries, the series aims to be transdisciplinary and includes works which combine, in different ways, such subjects as sociology, economics, politics and history in so far as they contribute to the understanding of cities.

The series also aims to contribute to cross-national understanding of cities. This is because, although Britain was the first country to experience a revolution in manufacturing industry, and the consequent industrial urbanisation, it has now reached a stage of de-industrialisation combined with de-urbanisation which needs to be set in an international context. The British economy is no longer in the world's first division. Events in its cities are increasingly determined by world rather than purely national economics. The understanding of this global context and how it is affecting cities in other countries is now an important part of urban analysis.

The series is also concerned with what private and public action should be recommended in cities. It is therefore interested in public and private policies with respect to cities and their regions.

The general aim of the series 'Sociology, Politics and Cities' is therefore to encourage and stimulate a continuing analysis of cities in capitalist, socialist and underdeveloped economies. It is concerned to develop theoretical understanding of these phenomena based upon empirical analyses. On the bases of such understanding the series is also concerned with the formulation and evaluation of relevant urban policies.

London 1985   James Simmie

Acknowledgements

The genesis of this book can be precisely located; it began when Dilys Hill, during the viva for my doctoral thesis, urged me to read in more detail the new urban politics literature. This I subsequently did, and discovered more of its treasures and pitfalls. I am, of course, very grateful to my supervisors at that time, Bill Hampton and Patrick Seyd, for their help in steering me through the hazardous exercise of thesis writing. It was due to them that I set about the long process of seeking a publisher. The end product, however, bears little resemblance to the thesis, although it was a vital stage in the intellectual preparation.

The first version of the text was written while I was working as a tutor organiser for the Workers' Educational Association in South Yorkshire; and it bore, at that stage, the hallmarks of that relatively isolated occupation. The current version has been formulated since I moved to the University of York, and became able to contact a wider academic community. Peter Saunders, Michael Harloe and Bill Hampton generously gave time to comment on drafts of the early chapters. Bill Hampton and Kathleen Jones kindly read at short notice the nearly complete text and made some very useful suggestions. Many thanks are due to James Simmie for suggesting how the first version could be made into a publishable commodity and trusting me to do the job. The creative environment generated by Kathleen Jones in the Department of Social Policy and Social Work has spurred me on. Our indispensable secretary, Alison Holdsworth, proof-read the manuscript and typed some of the draft version. I am very grateful to Janice Vanham for typing most of the draft and all of the final text.

But the greatest debt of all is owed to my family for making it possible for me to spend the hundreds of hours necessary to produce a book of this type.

January 1985   Stuart Lowe

Introduction

The previous two decades have seen the field of urban politics transformed from an institutionally rooted, eclectic specialism to a range of studies at the frontiers of our knowledge about the fundamental social and political processes in contemporary societies. Within this new literature an important sub-field, concerning the role of non-party urban movements as initiators of social change, rapidly emerged and now holds a central place in the debates. This theme reflected the abundant and diverse reality of urban protest across the globe, ranging from the black ghetto riots in the USA in the 1960s, to the squatter movements based in the shanty towns of rapidly urbanising societies, to the neighbourhood movement in Spain at the termination of the Franquist era, to the urban protest (particularly the mass movement of tenants) in Italy in the mid-1970s, to the less violent and less intense experience of the council house tenants' movements, redevelopment action groups and environmental organisations that were and remain a familiar feature of city politics in Britain. What do these movements and organisations represent? What effect have they had on social structures and in the policy arena? To what extent does their existence suggest a collapse of the formal procedures of political systems in expressing social conflict? Are there any similarities of experience across the globe that indicate the existence of common 'urban' processes irrespective of economic and political systems? Under what circumstances do people mobilise around urban issues and, by the same token, what factors inhibit or screen out potential urban protest? This book is addressed to these questions. It is focused mainly on Britain, as one country with a particular set of experiences, but the cross-national setting is integral to the approach.

Among the research workers and writers who fashioned the new urban politics, the figure of Manuel Castells is dominant. His book, *The Urban Question*, remains the most discussed and influential work of the new literature because in it are the foundations of a distinct 'urban' sociology: a field divorced from the institutionally contained urbanism thesis of the Chicago School (Park, Burgess, McKenzie, 1925; Wirth, 1928, 1938), which was the only other school of sociology to have identified a distinctively urban subject matter. Writing initially from within a continental neo-Marxist school, associated with the structuralist philosopher Althusser, Castells condemned all previous urban sociology as ideological, and reconstructed a new subject field which saw the urban system not as the location of geographically contained social processes, but as the focus of political conflict based on state intervention into the provision of key public services. The 'urban' was defined as the arena of the 'collective consumption' process. The significance of this at the political level was, as Castells saw it, that the urban was a focal point of a range of new challenges to the dominant capitalist order, matching the industrial class struggle as a fundamental source of social change. Within this conflictive process, Castells pointed particularly to the significant role of 'urban social movements' as harbingers of the transformation of the social relations of society. In its initial formulation, urban social movements, in alliance with the advanced sections of the working-class movement, were to create a revolutionary change in the distribution of power away from capitalist interests and towards socialism. Urban sociology was thus no longer a small, if influential, sub-discipline of academic sociology but was the theoretical basis for new schools of thought and urban practices at the centre stage of social transformation.

Over a decade on from his radical text of 1972 (published in English in 1977), Castells produced a new English language work in which he candidly renounces his early position, particularly the idea that class struggle is the motor force of social change, and adopts a new set of propositions concerning urban social change. But in *The City and the Grassroots* (1983), Castells retains at the core of his analysis the concept of urban social movements as the originators of alternative political and cultural systems: indeed, urban social movements are disengaged from association with political parties as initiators of change and stand as autonomous organisations constantly generating the possibility of new 'meaning sytems'. Since Castells is a founding father of the new urban sociology, tracing the evolution in his thinking is likely to be productive as a means of exploring and reviewing the debate about the urban system and process.

But what are urban social movements? There has been some discussion about the precise meaning of the phrase. In this study, the meaning adopted is different from the relatively specialised usage of Castells. It is important at the outset to be clear about definitions. The term is used here to mean organisations standing outside the formal party system which bring people together to defend or challenge the provision of urban public services and to protect the local environment. The implication of these organisations as 'social movements' is that their objectives are undertaken collectively by the mobilisation of a distinct social base and that the momentum of their activity is towards changes in policy direction. The definition suggested by Dunleavy fits closely to this notion: 'The important elements here are the stress on collectivity and on the push towards change of some kind. An urban social movement must display these characteristics in organising around urban issues of collective consumption' (Dunleavy, 1980, p. 156). Dunleavy goes on to draw attention to the distinctive organisational style of these groups – their grassroots orientation and unhierarchical mode of organisation, their distance from and non-involvement in formal party politics, and their emphasis on direct action and protest tactics. It is on these grounds that it is possible to distinguish urban social movements from conventional pressure groups and voluntary associations. The pattern of genesis of urban social movements in this definition is characteristically the creation of an issue around a particular social base, that is to say an objectively identifiable population targeted by an urban policy agency or policy issue. Mobilisation around these bases by no means always occurs, and one of the key themes in the analysis of urban social movements is the uncovering of forces and processes that operate at the institutional level to screen out social conflict; the theme of non-action is most readily approached in the analytical field of urban protest movements.

There has been an upsurge of urban social movement activity in Britain over the last two decades. Specific organisations of this type include the council house tenants' movement (dating from the late 1960s), which opposed government restructuring of rents towards market levels and the introduction of means-tested rebates; the ratepayer organisations that emerged in the mid-1970s to promote private sector provision of urban services and the abolition of rates; a range of groups opposing public spending cuts, giving rise to organisations concerned to save village and local schools, to defend smaller hospitals against mergers into large-scale district hospitals; redevelopment action groups that emerged in every major population centre where urban renewal and slum clearance programmes threatened stable communities and good quality housing; the squatters' movement that developed, particularly in London, in the late 1960s and reached a peak in the mid-1970s, housing thousands of single young people and families in empty public and private sector property; organisations to defend and promote public transport; groups against road-widening schemes and the building of trans-urban motorways; groups emerging at the time of the Health and Safety at Work Act (1974) that had gained a new understanding of the effects of industrial pollution on local residents. The list is by no means comprehensive but it does indicate the range of groups in Britain that fall within our adopted definition of urban social movements. This range and intensity of movements marked a significant upsurge of political activism in the British context. However, it is also clear that what happened in Britian was but a small part of a much wider post-war escalation of urban protest throughout the world, with an intensification in the 1960s and 1970s. Chapter 6 is directed specifically towards discussing comparative urban social movements and explores the evidence for the existence of cross-national structuring of urban protest. As will be shown in Chapter 2, the core of Castells's 1983 text is directed towards developing a comparative, cross-cultural theory of urban social change which has urban social movements as its central mechanism.

In *The City and the Grassroots*, Castells completely reorientates his use of the theory of urban social movements. They are still at the centre of his ideas on urban-based social change, but now, among other things, must be autonomous from political parties and be more involved in creating new cultural settings and urban 'meaning'. The consistent elements in Castells's usage is this ability to achieve some fundamental type of social change. But in practice what he means by social change has undergone a metamorphosis in the period between *The Urban Question* and *The City and the Grassroots*. There are three main phases in his use of the term 'urban social movement' to date. Taken as a whole, Castells's use is a specialised one in the context of classifying organisational types on a spectrum of 'effects' achieved. We are faced, therefore, with two distinct ways of using the phrase: Castells's prescriptive definition, and the view adopted in this text of grassroots movements seeking to influence policy change by collective action. Pickvance argues that Castells has a prior claim to the concept and that the phrase 'urban social movements' should be used only in his sense of the term, i.e. groups that achieve social transformations (Pickvance, 1983, p. 9). Instead, Pickvance argues, generic phrases such as 'urban protest', 'urban conflict', 'urban struggle', or 'urban movement' should be used to describe all other kinds of urban protest activities. By this means definitional confusion will be avoided. Pickvance may be correct to caution us, but Castells's usage is so specialised and the range of groups identified, including those described above, is so distinct, that a dual meaning is necessary.

The problem is not as difficult as it might appear. Despite the theoretical weight behind Castells's urban social movement analysis, the reality is that there are very few actual examples. Castells himself now admits that the only occasion on which he attempted to validate empirically his early structuralist inter-pretation of urban social movements, the results were a 'major fiasco' (1983, p. 298). And in his recent text he describes only one example of a fully fledged modern period urban social movement. But there are serious doubts whether even this, the Madrid Citizens' Movement, is a valid case (see Chapter 2). The crucial point is that the concept of urban social movements, in Castells's epistemology, is *always* tied to 'practice' – to the tactics necessary to achieve 'effects' – and that his strategies, the tasks he sets urban social movements, and the objectives, radically change between the 1972 and the 1983 texts. It is unwarranted, therefore, to abstract only part of the thesis –

social transformation – and to claim that this justifies giving Castells's usage a unique place in the literature. The evidence for the practical existence of urban social movements of the type discussed by Castells is too slender. When the phrase 'urban social movement' is used in Castells's specialised meaning, this will be made clear in the text. Otherwise the term is used in the more generalised sense.

Chapters 1 and 2 contain a review and critique of Castells's work on urban social movements up to and including *The City and the Grassroots* (1983). Chapter 3 takes a number of themes from the previous chapters, particularly on the factors that structure the mobilisation process, which includes both action and non-action around urban social bases. What motivates people to take collective action in the sphere of public service provision or, by the same token, for conflict to be repressed or screened out of the political arena? The factors treated as particularly significant in the British context are the characteristics of the local political systems, the sociology of the social bases and the structuring of the urban political system by a range of pervasive ideologies. The importance of the broad economic framework in the process of mobilisation and the growth or demise of certain types of movement is recognised: conditions of economic expansion are likely to generate a different range of movements from conditions of recession and declining expectations. Chapters 4 and 5 contain case studies of urban social movements in Britain. The relative dearth of information about this type of movement partly reflects their low visibility and generally their outsider status, and partly reflects the fact that the local politics literature in Britain has a long tradition of institutionally rooted approaches (Dunleavy, 1980, Chapter 1). Major examples of the council house tenants' movement, ratepayers' associations and the squatters' movement are examined. These cases have been chosen to illustrate and develop the themes in the earlier chapters. In particular an attempt is made to show how the public/private sector divide, and the ideologies around it, give rise to specific forms of movement activity and institutional responses. They illustrate the mechanisms adopted by local state organisations to co-opt or repress urban conflict and the differential treatment afforded to the sectors, generally implying defence of the private sector.

Chapter 6 takes up the earlier discussion of the cross-cultural model or urban social change found in Castells's *The City and the Grassroots*. The themes from the British case study chapters are integrated into an analysis of the basis on which the comparative study of urban politics, and urban social movements in particular, can be made validly. The argument is critical of the modelling methodology adopted in recent work in this field, but does not imply the rejection of this methodology as part of a multi-faceted research agenda, in a field of enquiry that is still immature. The short Chapter 7 makes an evaluation of the contemporary state of the practice and meaning of urban social movements as conceived by Castells, summarises the arguments on the analytical basis of the study of urban social movements, and concludes with an application of this methodology to Britain in the mid-1980s.

Chapter 1

Castells on Urban Social Movements

For students of urban politics, the work of Manuel Castells has been a seminal influence for a period spanning two decades. His ideas on the definition of the subject field and content of the urban system and process have provoked the most important and far-ranging debate since urban studies first reached maturity as a distinct discipline in the work of the 'Chicago School' of sociologists in the 1920s. There are, of course, many other contributors to the new urban politics field, but Castells's texts are both qualitatively and quantitatively the most significant. Not all his material is available in English translation, and the review of his work in this chapter is limited to the articles and books that are more readily available to English readers. In addition, the philosophical genesis of Castells's original position has been more than adequately discussed elsewhere (Saunders, 1981).

The purpose of Chapters 1 and 2 is to describe the way in which Castells conceives and uses one of his core concepts, the theory of urban social movements. These movements stand at the centre of his thinking on the way in which the urban system generates political conflict and social change. But over the last ten years his position has undergone a series of revisions, culminating in his most recent major text, *The City and the Grassroots* (1983), in which he makes a *volte-face* on his theoretical perspective, a change arising out of a lengthy analysis of historical and contemporary urban social movements. It is towards understanding this breach in his thinking that these chapters are partly geared. They may be read, therefore, as a brief introduction to the evolution of Castells's thinking up to and including his 1983 book. But the primary function of Chapters 1 and 2 is to assess the relevance of the urban social movements thesis as an explanatory and evaluative concept for characterising the activity of urban movements in Britain and internationally. It is in the context of a review and critique of the way Castells defines and uses the notion of urban social movements that the later chapters in this volume are set.

In order, however, to understand the central place of urban social movements in both Castells's 'early' and 'late' writings, a basic sketch of his general position must be made at the outset. This will be followed by a section that deals more centrally with the politicisation of the urban, and the definition, role and function of urban social movements. Chapter 2 focuses on Castells's newly adopted cross-cultural theory of urban social change and evaluates the concept of urban social movements as a means of specifying and characterising non-party urban political movements in Britain.

The urban domain

Writing from within one of the leading schools of continental neo-Marxism (Althusserian structuralism), Castells formulated his early position around a critique of all previous social science approaches to the urban social system. He singled out for special attention the Chicago School of urban sociology because of its formative and enduring influence, and looked closely at Louis Wirth's famous 'urbanism as a way of life' thesis; Castells regarded this as the best social science attempt to identify a specific theory of urban sociology. 'Urbanism' was rejected by Castells because the cultural systems claimed to be fashioned out of city life are not caused by factors specific to the city, but are general products of capitalist society as a whole. Urbanism, in Castells's parlance, was not a 'real object'. Furthermore, Castells claimed that the urbanism thesis in fact implies an historical process of transformation from folk to urban society, suggesting that modern society (industrial capitalism) is the end product of a natural process of development.

> Urbanism is not a concept. It is a myth in the strictest sense, since it recounts ideologically, the history of mankind. An urban sociology founded on urbanism is an ideology of modernity ethnocentrically identified with the crystallization

of the social forms of liberal capitalism. (Castells, 1969, in Pickvance (ed.), 1976, p. 70)

In his most recent work Castells recaptures more than a little of the urbanism thesis in his reconstituted theory of urban social change when he calls for the defence of cultural identity and the creation of autonomous local cultures. In his early position, however, urbanism was regarded as part of the ideological structuring of capitalism. But if the notion of an 'urban' sociology is to be retained (as distinct from a sociology of mass society in general) what, then, is its content, its 'real object'? And how, assuming there is a subject matter, is it to be theorised? It is here that Castells introduced two notions that he claimed constituted the real object of a reconstructed urban sociology; social relationships of space, and his notion of the process of collective consumption.

The division and use of space is a familiar and central part of much previous 'urban' sociology and human geography (Park, 1929; Christaller, 1933; Lösch, 1939; Hawley, 1950; Shefsky and Bell, 1955), which often focuses on a broadly ecological approach in which population, environmental, organisational and technological factors will relate to produce particular types of socio-spatial systems. Castells rejects these approaches because they too are ideological. They are ideological because in the realm of everyday experience space exists only in so far as it is mediated by social relations: 'Socially speaking, space, like time, is a conjuncture, that is to say, the articulation of concrete historical practice' (Castells, 1977, p. 442). Each historical era redefines space according to the dominant social order prevailing at the time. Under monopoly capitalism, Castells argues, the function of space is to serve the economic organisation of industrial production; a scale of activity that transcends the city and is ultimately global in its extent.

But production is only one half of the classical Marxist analysis of the capitalist economy. The other half of the equation is the requirement, first, for goods to be consumed, and second, within this generalised consumption process, for the industrial labour force itself to be replenished and of functional use at the point of production. In Marxism the process of providing life-sustaining facilities – such as housing and food – is referred to as the 'reproduction of labour power'. Under modern conditions a degree of literacy and health care, together with other public services, are also a necessary part of this process and have partly been won by the labour movement as a concession for social stability. Schools, hospitals, transport services and leisure amenities are all part of the means of ensuring that there is an available, mobile and compliant workforce. The reproduction of labour power and the 'extended reproduction of labour power' (the term used to described the broader range of necessary services) together are achieved by private and public provision, and are referred to by Castells as the 'means of consumption'. According to Castells, it is in the urban system that these consumption processes are located. The organisation of space to achieve the reproduction of labour power is the defining characteristic of the urban domain.

This definition has been widely criticised, particularly for making an apparently artificial separation between the production and consumption systems. Harloe, for example, argues that '"Urban" processes and forms cannot be understood without reference to the production of capital, and the reproduction of the labour force' (Harloe, 1977, p. 22). But Castells clearly did not intend to divorce the two processes, and simply argued that the urban has a particular specificity arising out of its spatial and functional relation to the 'everydayness' of workers' experience which might be defined by, for example, commuting movements. Against this, the production functions of capital are, as we have seen, at least regional and often national and international in scale. There is no question or intention of suggesting that the capitalist process is made up of mutually exclusive spatial or functional units. Castells wished to argue that the consumption process is what characterises the urban domain. And there is a second reason for this specialisation, which is a core element in Castells's perspective. For various reasons, which will be discussed later, in modern capitalist societies the processes involved in the reproduction of labour power are increasingly provided by the state in a collective form: 'the urban refers not only to a spatial form but expresses the social organisation of the process of reproduction' (Castells, 1977). Collective provision necessarily leads to a degree of centralisation of service administration, and this factor also enhances the spatial dimension of the notion of the urban. Local authority boundaries might be taken, therefore, as another experiential division of the urban system.

State intervention into the consumption process is an enduring and central theme in Castells's work, but the way he theorises state action evolves from an original position rooted in structuralism. The evolution in his thinking on the state also feeds into his ideas on the politicisation of the urban system, and for this reason the next sub-section provides a rudimentary account of the structuralist influence, particularly as it is advanced by Althusser.

Structure, class struggle and the state

It would be impossible to describe in detail here the structuralist proposition. Comments are confined to those elements of structuralism that are crucial to understanding the way Castells uses it, and readers are referred to the text by Althusser and Balibar (1970) for a more detailed exposition.

Althusser argues that Marx, in a number of his 'late' period documents, suggests that the clash between labour and capital is not sufficient on its own to create a social revolution; that the economic level, although dominant, creates, and is in its turn affected by, ideological and political factors. Around this 'discovery' Althusser constructs an enormously complex theoretical position. The important point here is that within the overall unity of the primary economic system a matrix of secondary contradictions are set up within, and between, these three fundamental social system elements – the economic, the ideological and the political levels. It follows from this that social transformation is no longer guaranteed by the simple capital/labour clash but depends on a set of circumstances in which issues from within the three levels 'fuse into a ruptural disunity' (Althusser, 1969, p. 116). Castells argues that it is within the urban system that new sources of contradictions are located arising from the necessary intervention by the state into the process of the reproduction of labour power. The social system structure determines the need and nature of state intervention because the state – as taught by Althusserian structuralism – within the political level, has the specific function of regulating the total system and ensuring its continued unity under the hegemony of capital.

The problem here is to describe exactly how the state and the total social structure interact. Althusser's system was criticised for being too mechanistic and for dissolving all trace of human influence from events. Structure could not determine all. Responding to this problem Castells drew on the work of Poulantzas to describe and theorise the state/social system connection. Poulantzas takes from the unadulterated structuralist position the view that the state has the specific function of regulating the total social system. But as part of the total system the state must itself be subject to the effects of system contradictions (Poulantzas, 1973). Here Poulantzas modifies and develops the crude structuralist model by arguing that there is a second level of determination, other than structure, within the social system, namely class struggle. Class struggle, he argues, in part arises out of system contradictions and feeds back into the state itself and determines to some extent how the state functions and creates policy. The state has, therefore, a degree of autonomy – a 'relative autonomy' – because it is not the unmediated functionary of the dominant social system, and at any one time may intervene against the immediate interests of a particular fraction of capital and may make concessions to non-capitalist interests as a means of regulating the class struggle. It is through this line of argument that Poulantzas accounts for the growth of welfare states and increased spending on social consumption.

The influence of the dual notions of structure and class struggle are fundamental to Castells, at least until very recently. But as Saunders points out, Castells shifts his early position away from the necessary (structurally determined) functions of the state to an emphasis on the determinant effects on the state of class struggle (practice). Saunders goes on to argue that the theory of the state used by Castells is nevertheless still flawed because

it fails to relate structures to practices and the functional requirements of the system to the effects of class struggle, and this means that the shift in emphasis from the former (functions and structures) to the latter (class struggle and practices) merely reproduces the problem and does not solve it. (Saunders, 1981, p. 190)

As we shall see, Castells's most recent work abandons completely the notion of the determinant effects of structure and class struggle as it is conceived in the Poulantzean manner. This is not to say that Castells has dropped any idea of structure, but in his new theory the emphasis is on structures based around metaphors of city life and 'urban meaning'. This does nevertheless mark an absolute break in his theoretical perspective.

We have now assembled the basic elements of Castells's original position: (a) The redefinition of the urban in terms of the social relations of space and as the arena for the process of the reproduction of labour power; (b) the intervention of the state as a provider of 'collective consumption' facilities arising from contradictions in the social system; and (c) the determinant effects of structure and class struggle on state action, with a tendency to shift towards the latter as the key influence. Castells holds both elements in his theoretical position via the Poulantzean notion of 'relative autonomy'. In the next section Castells's understanding of the political effects created by state intervention into the urban system and process is discussed.

Politicisation of the urban system

The significance of state intervention in the process of the reproduction of labour power is seen by Castells not only as a functional requirement of mature capitalist economies, but also as the source of a range of contingent problems and issues:

> The contradictions it [monopoly capitalism] developed in the sector of collective goods and services leads to an intervention by the state which, far from regulating the process, exacerbated contradictions and politicised the issue. (Castells, 1978a, p. 174)

The more the state becomes embroiled in the provision of public services, the more intense and dramatic become the possible political repercussions. These stem largely from the fiscal crisis that massive state spending ultimately generates, and the penetration of consumption services and issues into every corner of daily life. Disengagement from such deep-level public spending programmes is difficult without either raising taxes to an unacceptably high level or causing the possibility of social instability because of protest action by consumers and public sector workers against cuts in services. Resistance to cuts is heightened because state spending has the historic effect of establishing new horizons for working-class demands based on the 'social wage'.

However, the politicisation of the urban system must not be seen as an accident because (from the point of view of the dominant classes) state intervention in the consumption arena is a necessary product of the evolution of the capitalist economy. The central factor involved here concerns the need for an increasingly compliant and adaptable workforce in the face of highly integrated modern production methods.

> The growing importance of the predictability of the behaviour of labour power in a complex and interdependent production process requires increasing attention to the collective treatment of the processes and its reproduction. (Castells, 1977, p. 462)

The significance of state intervention in the urban system in Castells's work, at least until the late 1970s, is held, therefore, between two contrasting forces. On the one hand is the functional requirement for the control and stabilisation of the workers, which is largely achieved within the consumption sphere (because concessions are more easily and less dangerously made outside the factories), and on the other hand expanding expectations through the social wage and new sources of protest are both generated by state policy. The demand for an increasingly regulated urban process is encapsulated by Castells in what he calls the 'theme of urban planning'. The converse theme, of protest and dissent by consumers, is specified as the 'theme of urban social movements'. But as Dunleavy points out, there has been a methodological problem in the relationship between these two core themes. The tendency has been to look at one or the other, 'but with relatively poor levels of integration between the two' (Dunleavy, 1980, p. 48). The point here is that the politicisation of the urban does not simply imply an intensification of the class struggle, although it can do in certain circumstances, and may be understood equally as a source of social control.

> Politicisation thus established is not necessarily a source of conflict or change for it may also be a mechanism of integration and participation. Everything depends on the articulation of the contradictions and practices or, to put it another way, on the dialectic between the state apparatus and urban social movements. (Castells, 1977, p. 463)

What exactly does Castells mean when he draws our attention to the 'articulation of contradictions and practices' as crucial factors in assessing the political effects created within the urban system? There are several key points here which lead us into his precise definition and usage of the term urban social movements (and should not be confused with his 'theme of urban social movements', which is his general description for the whole sub-field of urban-based political organisation and protest). First of all, a point that has been rehearsed to some extent in the previous section concerns the nature of urban issues as 'secondary contradictions' within the social system. The primary class conflict takes place at the level of the economic; this is the dominant level involving, under capitalism, the clash between labour and capital. Secondary structural issues, following the Althusserian method, do not necessarily confront directly this fundamental power system. The point, however, is that collective consumption issues – the secondary issues of this instance – can in certain circumstances be thrust into a central role in the anti-capitalist struggle. Everything depends on the balance of class forces in a particular conjuncture and the extent to which the primary structural level is, in structuralist language, 'overdetermined'. Speaking of the centrality of the capital/labour confrontation in the social system, Castells says,

> But this does not mean that urban struggles are necessarily relegated to the world of administrative reformism. Quite the reverse; their decisive importance in certain political conjunctures has been determined, for a structurally secondary issue

can be a conjuncturally principal one. This means that the political importance of an urban movement can only be judged by relating it to the effects it has upon the power relations between social classes in a concrete situation. (Castells, 1977, p. 377).

The significance of urban issues is contingent, therefore, on whether or not they can decisively affect the balance of power between the classes and therefore break from their status as secondary contradictions. For this to happen the issues must, of course, be the expression of a contradiction within the social system structure in which definite 'stakes' (that is, socially based material interests) are present. It is in this context, of organisations in the urban system with a clear issue-base and capable of creating a shift in the balance of class forces, that Castells speaks of urban social movements.

The notion of urban social movements as qualitatively higher and more politically advanced than other organisations and capable of producing system change is a relatively consistent theme in Castells's writing. But the precise tactics necessary to this end undergo a series of adaptations and developments which run parallel and interact with his general theorisation of the urban process. Although the lines of discontinuity are not sharply drawn, there are three main phases in the strategies Castells deploys in relation to urban social movements. The first two phases will be discussed in the following sub-sections, while the third will be dealt with in Chapter 2. The focus in that chapter is on his recent text, *The City and the Grassroots*, where, as we have intimated, a much sharper break does occur in his theoretical position.

Urban social movements – phase one

In his early articles and texts, we must recall again, Castells locates his theoretical position within formal structuralism. The dominant level is the economic and the primary contradiction in society is between capital and labour at the point of production. In this context it follows that urban social movements – organisations that consciously and materially alter the balance of class forces in society – can only be generated if they can be linked to the dominant level. As secondary contradictions there is no possibility of urban movements, on their own, being able to produce 'effects' that change the structure of social relations.

> there is no qualitative transformation of the urban structure that is not produced by an articulation of the urban movements with other movements, in particular (in our societies) with the working class movement and the political class struggle. (Castells, 1977, p. 453)

At this stage Castells is arguing that urban movements are only capable of becoming urban social movements if they are drawn into the advanced sections of the working-class movement. This is because the only way contradictions in the total social system can be linked is through the mediation of a political organisation following a 'correct line' (which in general means relating an awareness of structure to a consciousness of the state of the class struggle and therefore become capable of leading).

> The role of organization (as a system of means specific to an objective) is fundamental, for . . . it is the organization that is the locus of fusion or articulation with other social practices. When there is no organization, urban contradictions are expressed either in a refracted way, through other practices, or in a 'wild' way, a pure contradiction devoid of any structural horizon. (Castells, 1977, pp. 271–2)

Urban social movements in this specification have a special place in the political system because they generate new areas of confrontation in the anti-capitalist struggle. By the same token other forms of protest movement within the urban problematic, those that do not connect to the advanced working-class movement, are by definition incapable of producing sustained 'effects' on the balance of class forces. More than that, protest groups play precisely the role intended by the dominant system by deflecting social discontent away from the primary class conflict and into the urban system. Castells constantly warns of the ideology of 'the urban' as a source of mystification; it is a theme he develops more strongly in his more recent texts. At this earlier stage his position is uncompromising. Either urban movements create social change (i.e. they become an urban social movement) or they become 'instruments of participation within general, dominant institutional objectives' (Castells, 1977, p. 378).

This was Castells's position on urban social movements in 1972 when the first four parts of *The Urban Question* were published (in French). But by the time of the English edition, published in 1977, Castells had added a fifth part and an extended 'Afterword'. Part Five is based on studies made by Castells in the United States. In it, and in other articles written at about this time (1975), his hard line is beginning to soften. In particular, in relation to urban social movements, he now adds a new dimension: that urban protest is important because it potentially links different social classes, especially middle to working class. This is because urban issues cross-cut the basic class divisions affecting people as a result of exposure to common consumption problems and issues. Health care or education are necessary *public* facilities for all but the most wealthy. As Castells says,

'Urban' social contradictions . . . are of a 'pluri-class' nature, in the sense that the cleavages they effect do not correspond to the structural opposition between the two fundamental classes, but rather distribute the classes and fractions in a relation whose opposing terms vary widely according to the conjuncture. It is deduced from this that 'urban politics' is an essential element in the formation of class alliances, in particular in relation to the petty bourgeoisie. (Castells, 1977, pp. 432–3)

Building cross-class alliances thus becomes an important part of Castells' strategy for urban politics and marks an important development from his original position based on the hegemony of the working class. It is a theme that was strengthened in his next major text to appear in English.

Urban social movements – phase two

The problems associated with the structural determination of social change, and in particular the way in which Castells theorised secondary contradictions (and the 'urban' within that level) began to produce significant changes of emphasis in his position in the mid-1970s. His view of urban social movements entered a completely new phase that had been, to some extent, prefaced in Part Five of *The Urban Question*. The key text in this period is his *City, Class and Power* (1978a), which is a collection of articles and essays written between 1971 and 1977. But in new material – the Introduction and concluding chapter – Castells updates his general perspective and begins to look forward to a major re-working of his analysis of the urban system. In this section the main developments in the 1978 book are evaluated and a short case study of an urban social movement in Madrid, also published in 1978 (Castells, 1978b), is also considered.

There are two main areas of development in the text. These concern, first, adaptations to his general theorisation of the urban, and, second, a new formula for the politicisation of the revised urban system. Under the first heading the key change involves the identification of new forms of social cleavage arising from collective consumption but *not* dependent on the class system *per se* for their existence in the social system, or as a source of political conflict.

> our hypothesis is precisely that . . . there is a new source of inequality in the very use of these collective goods which have become a fundamental part of the daily consumption pattern. (Castells, 1978a, p. 16)

This makes quite explicit the point that was emerging towards the end of *The Urban Question*. In an article from 1975, Castells uses this analysis to upgrade his initial reading of urban issues within the structural level of secondary contradictions. They do not supplant the primary capital/labour contradiction, but he now reaches a point where there is much greater parity between the two levels:

> we are not proposing the replacement of the labour/capital contradiction which defines the working class by a new principal contradiction defined in the sphere of socialised consumptions; rather, it is the deepening of a secondary structural contradiction and the new historical role it can play through social movements and the processes of change it can potentially provoke. (Castells, 1978a, p. 127)

This position points also to the second area of development in the 1978 book, concerning the politicisation of the urban. Here Castells suggests that urban-based movements may have an *autonomous* role in social change, a role that his earlier model of urban political conflict (based solely on the linkage of secondary contradictions to the working-class movement) vigorously denied. It clearly follows that if there are non-class-based consumption stakes, then there can equally as well be consumption-based political movements that do not depend on the mediation of a vanguard party to achieve political 'effects'; although at this stage Castells does not in fact draw out the complete logic of this position.

What is the basis on which Castells arrives at these rectifications to his perspective? He focuses his thinking here on a number of long-term structural tendencies in advanced capitalism; the concentration and centralisation of capital and its battle against the tendency for the rate of increase of profit to decline, developments in the class struggle – particularly the growing power of the labour movement – and above all the massive and sustained intervention of the state into the whole economic sphere in both production and consumption. More specifically Castells points to the need for new markets which entails the opening up of the consumption sphere to the widest possible social strata. At the same time the workers' movement has pushed forward the historic definition of need, in large measure because consumption-based demands can be more easily and less dangerously accommodated by the dominant classes than demands for political power-sharing or demands at the point of production. New technology, in addition, has heightened the significance of collective consumption provision because industrial production systems are more integrated and taut, requiring an absolutely smooth functioning factory routine; thus a specialised worker can easily be replaced but an effective transport system is essential to move manpower to the factory routinely. As Castells suggests,

> the more important constant capital becomes in its size and in relation to the labour power, the more essential its smooth functioning becomes in rendering cybernetic the most unpredictable element of the productive process, i.e. the workers. (Castells, 1978a, p. 17)

Consumption processes are, therefore, of crucial importance in advanced capitalism, partly to generate the utilisation of capital accumulation and partly as a means of creating an efficient industrial system. These factors are the source of a major contradiction in the economic system arising from the increasing interdependence of the public and private sectors in regulating the functioning of the economy in the interests of the domination of private capital. It is the role of the state to regulate this process, and so the state itself becomes more totally involved in preparing conditions that are favourable to capital, by ensuring the necessary reproduction of labour power at minimum acceptable cost, by directing its own spending in favour of the private sector, and by preparing the conditions for the maximisation of private sector advantages (e.g. in land-use planning).

Castells suggests that out of this situation, in which collective consumption plays a crucial part, new sources of contradictions arise. In particular, Castells identifies a variety of sectoral cleavages based on the private and public provision of collective goods and services. These cleavages are most apparent in the consumption spheres of housing and transport, because both these areas are characterised by a major public/private divide. In the transport field,

> for the mass of wage-earners, the tendency is towards the growing spatial diffusion of activities, to the separation more and more strongly evident, between residence, work, recreation, shopping, etc., and thus to an increased daily dependence on the means of transportation. Such a dependence sets up new cleavages and gives rise to new contradictions. (Castells, 1978a, p. 29)

The division here is between private car ownership and reliance on the public transport network, with a tendency for people to combine the two methods. But the public system, operating at a minimum standard of comfort and services, creates the conditions for an expanding private car market and an ideology of individual freedom. Inequalities between types of car and between the public/private divide thus become sources of new inequalities, partly determined by income but partly cutting across the social classes. The provision of collective consumption in the context of the supremacy of the market system tends, therefore, to underline class stratification but creates also sectoral cleavages.

As Castells observes,

> aside from these effects of reinforcing the class structure, one finds new disparities, emerging from the historical mode of dealing with collective consumption, *which do not correspond to the position occupied in class relationships but to the position in the consumption process itself.* (Castells, 1978a, p. 34, emphasis added)

This perspective marks an important development in Castells's relationship with his early structuralism and the relative autonomy thesis, because he now admits a level of determinacy in distributing collective consumption from within the state, which is neither structurally determined nor determined by the class struggle. His discussion of the factors involved in access to public housing, for example, is reminiscent of the urban managerialist position (Pahl, 1975; Rex and Moore, 1967), and, as we shall see in Chapter 3, the notion of sectoral consumption cleavages is the source of an important analytical perspective based on a neo-pluralist school (Dunleavy, 1980).

This is not to say that Castells has yet abandoned the crucial role of class struggle in determining how the state acts: 'The action of the state is the result of a political process which is still largely determined by the class struggle' (1978a, p. 170). The state as the key manager of collective consumption provision – now a deep-level aspect of society – is responding to contradictions in the economic system (providing necessary services and infrastructure, regulating the economy, providing new markets), but in doing so politicises urban issues and in the process reveals the class-based nature of state policy. State action at this stage in Castells's work is seen mainly as a response to class conflict and is less centrally located in the logic of structural contradictions. As Saunders suggests, the elements of structure and practice are still the bedrocks of Castells's position. What has changed is the much stronger emphasis he now gives to the determinant effect of class struggle (Saunders, 1981, Chapter 6).

Finally, as suggested earlier, the position adopted in the 1978 book indicates a heightened significance for urban issues in the social system. This arises because capitalism progressively becomes more dependent on the collective consumption sphere, for the reasons outlined above.

The identification by Castells of consumption cleavages that cross-cut the class system, the growing importance of state intervention in the collective consumption process, and the upgrading of urban issues in the wider context of political struggle have two major consequences for his analysis of urban-based political movements:

1. a growing emphasis on the 'pluriclass' nature of urban politics; and
2. a change in the manner in which urban social movements and their strategic role in the anti-capitalist stuggle are theorised.

Politicisation in the new urban system

In his earlier texts, Castells stresses the point that the politicisation of the urban system is of potential significance because it provides the basis of inter-class alliances, particularly for a middle-class/working-class linkage. But at that stage the emphasis was on pulling the middle classes behind the working-class movement, arising from the contention that the anti-capitalist struggle must be led by the politically advanced sections of the labour movement:

> the key problem is then to unite the broader masses around an anti-monopoly political programme, that is to say, to con-struct the historical bloc of the dominated classes *under the hegemony of the proletariat*. Urban problems then play a privileged role in the construction of the class alliance based on protest (not only physical). (Castells, 1977, p. 465, emphasis added)

In *City, Class and Power*, however, the notion of proletarian hegemony gives way to a new political alternative, 'the democratic road to socialism'. This is a well-known slogan of the Eurocommunist movement which won growing support elec-torally in France and Italy in the 1970s, and led to a breakdown of relations between the European Communist Parties and Moscow. In Britain the Communist Party split around this question, with the hard-line 'Stalinist' wing rapidly shrinking into a small but still influential sect. Castells clearly feels that Eurocommunism is the strategy most appropriate to his analysis. His identification of consumption cleavages served to strengthen the view that cross-class movements were of potentially great significance and had the merit, in the context of the new political strategy, of drawing a wider social spectrum into the democratic socialist alliance. He points in particular to the significant role in urban issues played by 'the new petty bourgeoisie', who had for the first time become aware of the state as an antipathetic influence in society. Castells does not now talk of working-class hegemony but emphasises the need for popular unity, with a key role played by the professionals and salaried workers:

> the working class cannot on its own, in the 1970s, pose a socialist alternative in Western Europe . . . while the working class remains a fundamental axis of the Socialist project, the social strata essential in broadening the basis for its realisation are the salaried classes. (Castells, 1978a, p. 172)

There is now no question of a revolutionary assault on state power, but rather a gradualist infiltration of the state apparatus, and the building of popular political support for socialist parties, mainly via the ballot box.

In these circumstances Castells had much less to say about urban social movements, at least in his original specification, because urban-based protest movements that he had previously written off as reformist (and therefore in fact sustaining the dominant system) have gained a new status in the strategy of building the popular front. His use of urban social movements in this phase is ambiguous, because his original conception loses its relevance once the hegemony of the workers' movement is questioned. If the vanguard party is no longer central to the strategy, then the linkage of urban movements to it is no longer necessary.

The way in which Castells uses the notion of urban social movements in the late 1970s is perhaps best seen in his case study of the Citizens' Movement in Madrid (Castells, 1978b). Although he discusses this movement under the title 'Urban Social Movements and the Struggle for Democracy', nowhere in the article does he actually use the phrase, preferring to refer to the Citizens' Movement as 'The Movement'. This 'movement' consists of not one, but a plurality of different groups with different social bases, but united by a common concern with urban issues, such as housing, planning, the environment, 'lifestyle' and 'representation of the people'. The groups range from shanty-town and public housing movements to suburban and 'exclusive residential neighbourhood' organisations. Castells sees these groups as a movement in the sense that they were central organisations in the building of a popular anti-monopolist alliance, and all demanded the establishment of a democratic state (the genesis of the movement being the events surrounding, and the aftermath of, Franco's death). But what Castells is describing is not a pluriclass movement but a plurality of separate organisations. He himself makes the point that:

> although the Citizens' Movement is inter-class, the majority of its components tend to be homogeneous in class content. So the workers' neighbourhoods mobilize workers and the middle-class neighbourhoods mobilize separately. (Castells, 1978b, p. 143)

This is a long way from the middle-class/working-class linkage of Castells's earlier studies. In addition, he moves in the Madrid case study into a new realm of subjectivity by arguing for the creation of a 'new type of city' based on the breaking down of the anonymity and de-personalised relationships of city life. In a tentative way he begins now to speak of an idealised notion of urbanism, suggesting a degree of retrenchment from his original critique of the concept of urbanism. He discusses the struggles for community, individualism and new cultural forms, and in so doing must be considered to have broken completely with structuralism. It is clear, however, in the 1978 texts and essays that Castells is beginning to move not only beyond structuralism, but even beyond class struggle as the primary determinant of social change. This is apparent because he stresses the role of elections and popular control *outside* the mediation of political parties. For example, in the Madrid study he says, 'The Citizens' Movement complements the political parties, and permits citizens without a party to meet and participate in public life' (1978b, p. 145). This is a straightforward, orthodox statement that could have come from any number of advocates of 'public participation' in the late 1960s and 1970s. Castells emphasises that urban movements should be *autonomous* with regard to political parties. Linkage to any party, let alone left-wing parties, is opposed. The Citizens' Movement in Madrid, he asserts,

> believe that only if its political and ideological pluralism is preserved can it become a unified mass movement, which is what the population of Madrid needs. And only in this way can it be a key element in a grassroots democracy which will complement a representative democracy based on political parties and state institutions. (1978b, p. 146)

There is very little left here of a class-based analysis of social change, and this short article presages the *volte-face* that occurs in 1983 in his major text, *The City and the Grassroots*.

A second theoretical level that emerges out of the shift in Castells's position away from the structuralist influence is the recognition that different societies are subject to different historical processes and a differing arrangement of class forces, particularly in relation to the role and function of the state.

> The state is the expression of society, and thus both the crystallization of the historical process, and the expression of contradictory social relations which are at work in each period and in each social formation. (Castells, 1978a, p. 180).

Once the notion of structure as the overriding influence on state action is questioned, the way is clear to discuss the historical determination of the class struggle and politics in general across the whole spectrum of societies. This leads Castells to suggest that research into the role and function of the state and urban contradictions might more profitably start from a 'theorised history of states' rather than a general theory of the state *per se.* The problem of specifying the relationship between structure and practice is to be answered by developing a comparative model of forms of state intervention in the urban system. The 'historical problematic' is seen as the way forward to the specification of a new urban science. *City, Class and Power* concludes with a clear statement of intent to begin again his investigation into the place of urban contradictions in the process of social change, but now anchored to a generalised historical perspective and using case studies drawn from social and political contexts that most clearly articulate the theme of social change. Hence the focus of this research is to be on urban social movements which stand at the centre of the urban process. Once again, the centrality of the urban as a motor of social change in Castells's thinking is apparent.

In the material published in the late 1970s, therefore, there are strong pointers to a new approach. First, there is the break with structuralism and the strong suggestion that class struggle is not the only source of social change. Second, there is Castells's interest in the role of the new petit bourgeoisie in politics, the ecology movement, cultural forms and struggles for 'community'. Third, there is the suggestion that urban movements should be autonomous from political parties if they are to have a decisive effect on social change. Fourth, there is Castells's call for an historical enquiry into the role that urban contradictions have played in social change, which should be the bedrock of a new theory and science of urban politics. It is in *The City and the Grassroots* (1983), a book of major dimensions, that Castells attempts to integrate and develop these themes into a new 'theory of urban social change'. The book contains a series of lengthy and detailed case studies drawn from a wide range of historical periods and cultural settings, followed by an exposition of the new theory – and within this a new specification of urban social movements. Once again, therefore, it is necessary to discuss briefly the basic content of Castells's general perspective in order to locate how he now conceives the theme of urban social movements, the third phase in the chronology.

Chapter 2
The City and the Grassroots

The discussion in these few pages could not possibly indicate the totality of the vast canvas that Castells paints in his new text. It is a work of some 300,000 words. The methodological appendices, endnotes and bibliography alone cover 100 pages. The substance of the book presents case studies of historical and contemporary urban movements and urban social movements, ranging from the revolution of the Communidades in sixteenth-century Castille, to the 1871 Paris Commune, to the Glasgow Rent Strike in 1915, the protests in the Parisian Grandes Ensembles in the 1960s and 1970s, the cultural movements and gay communities in San Francisco, the Madrid Citizens' Movement of the 1970s, and much more besides. At the end of all this Castells's new theoretical perspective is summed up into a 'cross-cultural theory of urban social change'.

First of all in this chapter, the essential features of Castells's new perspective are described. A consideration of a selection of his case studies illustrates how he uses this new approach. Particular attention is paid to the Madrid Citizens' Movement, as he sees this as the archetypal urban social movement, and his experience of working with and observing this movement is central to his current thinking. Some of the main additions that have been made to his position are discussed, particularly his re-introduction of the concept of community and the idea of a cross-cultural theory or urban social movements. Finally, a number of other features of the work are briefly considered: his attitude and perspective on the politics of gender, and his view of contemporary urban social movements as conveyors of new societies, but of themselves incapable of achieving social transformation. The cross-national and comparative issues are discussed more fully in Chapter 6.

Urban social change

To begin with we will concentrate on the manner in which Castells re-casts his theory of urban social change, arising out of his comparative/historical research. How does he now theorise the politicisation of the urban? And what did he discover in his case-study research that lead him to dispense with some of the cornerstones of his previous analysis?

The major areas of reformulation concern the way in which he now defines the 'urban' and, secondly, his understanding of the process of urban social change, in which the third phase specification of urban social movements is located.

The first step in the new analysis involves the way in which he theorises the urbanisation process; and we immediately confront a major shift in his position. Previously, it may be recalled, Castells related the division and use of space exclusively to the dominant mode of production, which under capitalism is the industrial system; and within this, the urban as the focus of the consumption process. To this he now adds the crucial element of social process. By this he means the conscious actions of individuals and social groups (as well as classes) in shaping the city in the image of their own choosing.

> technology per se or the structure of the economy itself are *not* the driving force behind the process of urbanization. Economic factors and technological progress do play a major role in establishing the shape and meaning of space. But this role is determined, as well as the economy and technology themselves, by the social process through which humankind appropriates space and time and constructs a social organization, relentlessly challenged by the production of new values and the emergence of new social interests. (Castells, 1983, p. 291)

In adopting this position, in which 'personal experience' and the 'relationship between people and urbanization' are paramount, Castells is responding to the critique of his earlier studies by students of urban sociology – Rex and Pickvance from the English school – who argued that the absence of any subjective understanding of the way in which people interpret their social places and roles (characteristic of the structuralist formulation) leads to an inadequate explanation of the structure of social relations and the process of mobilisation.

A second crucial area of change also surfaces explicitly in his work for the first time; this is the question of the historical context of the urbanisation process in particular societies. The clash of values and social interests are conditional upon, and conditioned by, history. This new interest Castells draws from the influence on him of American neo-pluralist sociologists who locate US urbanisation and the urban crisis of the 1960s and its aftermath in the specific historical context of American society – particularly focused on the problems of mobilising the American working class in the absence of a mass labour movement, and with the existence of a range of alternative cultural loyalties based on the split between home and work, and on ethnicity and race (Piven and Cloward, 1977; Katznelson, 1981).

These two factors, of social process and social history, feed into a key aspect of Castells's position change – a redefinition of the 'urban'. As we have seen, this was a relatively settled aspect of his previous analysis. It is no longer defined as the arena for the collective consumption process (although that remains *part of* the contemporary urban system) but is fundamentally about the role a city plays in the context of the particular historical stage of society: 'Urban is the social meaning assigned to a particular spatial form by a ... historically defined society' (1983, p. 302).

It may be noted here, *en passant*, that Castells uses the terms 'urban' and 'city' interchangeably in his text; this is an important alteration in the context of his previous perspectives. Indeed, the focus of the book is on cities and not on the 'urban' as such, and indicates a loosening of his earlier criticisms of spatial interpretations of the urban arena, which he previously held to be ideological. The notion of the 'city' is nowhere defined in the book.

Castells sees cities as the product not of predetermined economic functions but of an interaction between social classes, interest groups or individuals. Each city comes to have a particular 'meaning' as a result of the outcome of this conflict in which dominant interests imprint their image and functional purpose on the urban system and process. This is not a static situation because dominated groups, within the dominant mode or 'meaning', are resistant and form the basis of new social struggles to change urban meaning.

Urban meaning is the synthesis of the historical social form and the specific model or 'goal' of a city, and is fashioned out of the conflict between the different stakes and values held by different groups and actors. For example, the mediaeval city was defined by the dominant class of merchants as a *market*; Castells suggests that this means the city is a reflection of fundamental social, cultural and economic processes:

> it will mean street fairs and intense socializing, but it will also mean the commodification of economic activity, monetariza- tion of the work process, and the establishment of a transport network to all potential sources of goods and to all markets that may be expanded. In sum, *the historical definition of the urban is not a mental representation of a spatial form, but the assignment of a structural task to this form in accordance with the conflictive social dynamics of history*. (Castells, 1983, p. 302, emphasis added)

Urban meaning is underpinned by the particular functions a city has; so that, for example, a colonial centre will have as its basic function the military control of the territory. Capitalist cities have the functions of profit-making industrial production, collective consumption, the extraction of profit through land and house sales, the organisation of capital circulation through the financial institutions; cities may specialise in one or more of these core functions.

Finally, urban meaning and urban function combine to produce urban form, 'the symbolic spatial expression of the processes that materialize as a result of them' (p. 303). Skys- crapers, for example, not only provide accommodation for business headquarters or real estate investment, but 'are the cathedrals of the period of rising corporate capitalism' (p. 303).

The conflict over urban meaning is the new focus of Castells's urban politics; and the process of redefining, challenging and changing urban meaning is called urban social change. Accord- ing to Castells, there are four basic ways in which a change of urban meaning can take place. The first is when the dominant class, using its institutional power, decides to restructure an existing meaning; here he cites the case of erstwhile industrial cities becoming 'warehouses for unemployed minorities'. The second is when a dominated class achieves a revolution and subsequently changes urban meaning; for example, the deurbanisation of Havana following the Cuban Revolution, 'or the workers of Glasgow in 1915 impose housing as a social service, not as a commodity.' (Castells, 1983, p. 304). Third, a social movement may be able to develop its own 'meaning' over a particular area in contradiction to the interest of the dominant meaning; there are no clear examples here except some 'feminist schemes'. Fourth, a social mobilisation imposes a new urban meaning against the interest of the institutionalised urban meaning and dominant classes. It is here that Castells specifies the definition of his new generation of urban social movements: they are 'urban-orientated mobilizations that influence structural social change and transform the urban meanings' (p. 305). Castells is careful to suggest that all social change does not necessarily lead to changes of urban meaning; for example, some Eastern bloc societies retain the city as the focal point of a nondemocratic state system. The link between changes in urban meaning and urban social movements is vital. Following on from his 1978 text, Castells now makes explicit that he no longer regards class struggle as the crucial determinant of social change:

> although class relationships and class struggle are fundamental in understanding urban conflict, they are not, by any means, the only primary source of urban social change. The autonomous role of the state, the gender relationships, the ethnic and national movements, and movements that define themselves as citizen, are among other alternative sources of urban social change. (Castells, 1983, p. 291)

Urban social movements – phase three

The whole of Castells's previous position, certainly as it appears in *The Urban Question* based on urban issues as secondary contradictions in the social system, now gives way to a plurality of other primary sources of change. Castells goes on to classify these movements for social change into three main types arising from the particular goals that each pursues:

1. Groups involved in collective consumption issues that seek to build a notion of urban living based on the city as an entity concerned with need (use value) rather than for profit (exchange value).
2. Groups that fight to defend or create communities with a particular cultural identity; arising from historic or ethnic sources. The defence of 'inter-personal communication' is contrasted to the hegemony of the mass media in the arena of personal and community association. Movements orientated to this goal are called 'community movements' by Castells.
3. The goal of attempting to achieve local self-government and the decentralisation of service provision from the central state, the 'struggle for a free city', is undertaken by groups called 'citizens' movements'.

These three themes, of the relationships of consumption, of communication and of power are the new core of Castells's urban political analysis, and it is around them that he constructs his third phase urban social movements.

As with his original specification of urban social movements – organisations that can effect social change – so in their most recent form they are singled out for their ability to create a qualitatively new balance of relationships within the social system. But in this case the change that is required concerns the impact that can be made on 'urban meaning'. Organisations that achieve this do so as a result of synthesising in their practice the three elements of collective consumption demands, community culture and political self-management. Only organisations that interconnect these themes are capable of accomplishing a change of urban meaning. Urban social movements are defined as

> a collective conscious action aimed at the transformation of the institutionalized urban meaning against the logic, interest, and values of the dominant class. It is our hypothesis that only urban social movements are the urban-orientated mobilizations that influence structural social change and transform the urban meanings. (Castells, 1983, p. 305)

The political strategy on which these movements are based extends the 1978 position by insisting on the *separation* between urban social movements and political parties:

> while urban social movements must be connected to the political system to at least partially achieve its goals, they must be organizationally and ideologically autonomous of any political party. (Castells, 1983, p. 322)

The reasons for this insistence on political autonomy arise from his new reading of the social system reliant on social process, meaning here personal and group interaction, to achieve changes in values and meaning systems. To be able to implement value and meaning changes urban movements must be ideologically untainted by party programmes. Castells sees that political parties are bound into the 'political level', which refers in this text to the area defined previously by Castells as the theme of urban planning; broadly, it is the state apparatus operating in the terms of dominant social interests. On the other hand urban social movements relate to 'civil society', which is a separate level of the social structure in which dominant values and institutional norms are not necessarily accepted. This is why social movements are the genuine source of social change whereas political parties remain only at the level of political bargaining. But Castells is careful to argue that an open political system is necessary in order to permit the innovations proposed by urban social movements to be carried through.

> Without political parties and without an open political system, the new values, demands, and desires generated by social movements not only fade (which they always do, anyway) but do not light up in the production of social reform and institutional change. (Castells, 1983, p. 294)

Unfortunately this leads to an ambiguous conclusion that although urban social movements can innovate social change, they themselves cannot carry it through to a transformation of society because this depends on adaptations at the political level. This important theme is considered in Chapter 7.

The main themes of Castells's new position and his phase

three specification of urban social movements have now been described. How Castells has derived his model of urban social change and how he uses it will be more apparent in the context of a consideration of some of his case-study material. Within this discussion a number of lines of criticism will begin to emerge.

The case studies

Before commenting on the case-study material some discussion of the methodology adopted in *The City and the Grassroots* is necessary, because Castells argues an important relationship between his process of theory-building and his empirical data. There are problems with this methodology and the manner of his theorisation.

According to Castells, he started his research by looking at a number of key questions, 'themselves generated by the social issues arising from historical experience'. In fact he produced a screened list of questions, a set of hypotheses and a very carefully selected group of case studies. There must always, of course, be hypotheses in relation to a subject of enquiry, but Castells links his choice of case studies so closely to his initial hypotheses that his ultimate generalisations must be read with some caution. In his historical cases, for example, he has chosen some very dramatic but exceptional moments (and has written some fascinating accounts). But has he imposed an interpretation on the events to suit his preconceived notion of the conflictual processes in the battle for urban meaning?

In the case of the Glasgow Rent Strike in 1915, Castells suggests that 'the process of working class mobilization in Glasgow, and its powerful expression in the Rent Strike, seems to have been the immediate historical factor imposing a new housing policy against financial and real estate interests' (p. 27). This interpretation is a gross exaggeration of the significance of the strike. It was unquestionably a dramatic circumstance. Clydeside was the centre of the munitions industry and under war conditions 16,000 new workers came into Glasgow. Virtually all accommodation was privately rented and the landlords took advantage of the new scarcity to increase rents. At the same time the government had acted quickly to control trade union rights in order to ensure production for the war effort. Many of the men were away in the forces. There was also a close relationship between the industrial and the residential communities, and this factor, in particular, was unusual and a crucial source of strength for the rent strike that started in May 1915. It was ferociously fought, mainly by women, who were at the forefront of the issue. By November there were 25,000 people on rent strike, and with the very real possibility of the trade unions acting to support the strike (despite the war-time restrictions) a Bill was rushed through Parliament freezing rents at pre-war levels.

As Castells points out, this legislation was supported by many industrialists anxious in the long run to have their workforce adequately housed. The rentier class had tried to make excessive profits out of the consumption arena and the people rebelled against this over-exploitation. Pickvance (1982) rightly points to the convergence of interests surrounding the growth of reformist housing policy – the convenience of industrial capital, the militancy of the workers, and the war situation in which the government needed to ensure a constant and high level of munitions production. Moreover, at the end of the war it was politically unacceptable for the families of returning troops to be faced with a sudden bout of rent rises (Bowley, 1945). Some form of government subsidisation became a necessary component of housing policy.

Castells's understanding of the events is that they demonstrated the dominance of the capitalist relations of production, reluctantly accepted by the workers, whose demand was that the capitalist city should expand its urban meaning to include the welfare of the workforce. As he says, 'They wanted the city to be part of a social wage for them', but without challenging the core urban meaning and functions. The common ground was that the city should stay as the locus of production and a (socially and spatially) class-divided society. The impact of the Rent Strike was to add the notion of use-value to the functions of the capitalist city and, in general, to initiate early welfare state policies. Any notions of the city containing new cultural forms or new types of political control were outside the terms of this dispute. In the end the strikers won the issue, but did not succeed in challenging the fundamental power of the dominant class. This certainly is the case, but in what sense, then, is Castells discussing the Glasgow Rent Strike as an 'urban social movement'? It did not change the power relations of society, it did not develop new cultural meanings or initiate a movement for local self-government. What it did was to influence not 'urban meaning' but nationally structured housing policy. In short, measured by Castells's own prescription of an urban social movement, the Glasgow Rent Strike of 1915 matches up to only one of the four elements: the collective consumption factor. Indeed, in the generalised terms that Castells uses there are much better examples in this period of British housing policy of changes in urban meaning. For example, the rise of the building society movement in the 1920s led to an explosion of house building with new 'meaning' systems (privately owned), new urban symbolism (suburban housing capturing an ideal-ised rural/anti-urban lifestyle) leading to the collapse of private renting and dramatically realigning the social structure around individual property ownership. This was, of course, an example of a change of meaning created by a dominant class, but the effects were far more radical and sustained than the apparent consequences of the events in Glasgow in 1915. It can be argued, therefore, that there are problems in isolating apparently seminal events and attaching too much significance to them: it is an inherently unhistorical methodology. This is not to deny that some events are seminal, but there are alway interpretative issues.

The Citizens' Movement

Of the modern period case studies, by far the most detailed and important in the context of Castells's theory is the Madrid Citizens' Movement. It is, in his view, the archetypal urban social movement, and his thinking and conclusions on it ripple through his interpretation of all the other case studies. The Citizens' Movement is the example by which everything else is judged: 'we propose the structural formula we discovered in our research in Madrid as the general structural formula able to foster the fulfilment of an urban social movement across different cultures of the capitalist-informational mode of production and in our epoch' (p. 322).

Once again, however, there are conceptual problems and difficulties of historical interpretation. The key factor here is that the Citizens' Movement may well be a special case, but only because the historical circumstances of its origins were unique in the context of European history. First of all, what was the Citizens' Movement, what were its special features (the past tense is used advisedly because it no longer exists as an urban social movement in Castells's terms), and what were the circumstances surrounding its origins?

The movement emerged in the late 1960s in the context of a nationwide urban-based crisis caused by a combination of over-exploitation and domination of public services – housing in particular – by capitalist interests intimately linked to the Phalange Party machine, and by the gathering pace of opposition to the Franquist régime. In 1969 Franco instigated a particularly brutal purge of his opponents (declaring a 'state of exception') and dismantled all popular and uncontrolled organisations. In these circumstances the anti-Franquist forces were driven to building new and less obtrusive political forms around which to mobilise the anti-state movement. In Madrid the neighbourhood movement developed rapidly around a series of urban issues – housing, transport, health care – with different areas demanding different things. All of them in the end put forward demands for political democracy. Each group governed a specific area of the city and, because they were illegal organisations, acted very cautiously. But as Castells suggests, 'the very fact of their existence was a breakthrough for democracy against an authoritarian state' (p. 226). After Franco's death (in 1975) and the move towards a democratic state, the territorial link became a problem because the new democracy was based on political parties.

A major feature of the Citizens' Movement was its social and organisational diversity. In an article written in 1978, Castells calls the movement an 'inter-class' organisation. By this Castells does *not* mean class mixing but, rather, that each area had a class-defined social base which fed into individual groups. In other words, each group was an autonomous entity generally representing a particular class interest. It was a movement composed of a series of separate organisations. Castells identifies five main types:

1. 'Shanty town mobilizations' demanding basic facilities and ultimately renewal of the areas by publicly controlled urban redevelopment.

2. 'Public housing estate mobilizations' aimed at improving the appalling quality of construction and for the rebuilding of the worst estates.

3. 'Protests over the urban facilities in the privately developed, large housing estates'; these largely suburban areas contained both workers and middle-class people but both groups demanded access to urban facilities such as education, health care, water supply, roads, etc.

4. 'The revolt of the middle-class residential neighbourhoods'; these were upper middle-class suburban neighbourhoods discontented with an isolated lifestyle, lack of facilities and the overcrowding that developed as space was consumed for new development.

5. 'The preservation and revitalization of central Madrid'; developing in the mid-1970s, these groups opposed the speculative building and development of the central/historic area and of the downtown neighbourhoods which were being deliberately run down.

The fragmented character of the movement was initially its strength, because an amorphous body was difficult to control. Attempts to develop a federal, city-wide co-ordinating organisation were not successful, mainly because of the involvement in the Citizens' Movement of the Communist Party (PCE) and the Workers Revolutionary Organisation (ORT), who agreed to share power in the Federation. As Castells observes, 'participation in the Federation was a matter of politial discipline in which party instructions were to be followed rather than a belief in the Federation's usefulness to the Movement' (p. 229). Instead the movement maintained its diversified structure but overrode the Federation at city-wide level whenever necessary. Castells cites a number of large-scale protest demonstrations over issues such as the cost of living, a fraud in bread making, and the housing crisis. The Citizens' Movement was able to assert its existence as a non-party movement and 'an autonomous social force' (p. 230).

The territorial aspect of the neighbourhood associations was also important in this claim for autonomy. There was a constant tension for many of the activists in the movement, many of whom were also PCE or ORT members, between loyalty to their neighbourhood and loyalty to their party line. But the parties needed the large potential electoral base of support and the Citizens' Movement needed the activists to sustain and organise the local groups. However, following the death of Franco and the general process of liberalisation in Spanish society the movement reached a crisis. With a freer political atmosphere more groups developed or came into the open representing an expansion in the social cross-section of the movement and the issues it represented. But, at the same time, and because of its expanding social base and the important role played in its leadership by party political activists, 'it entered into a series of major conflicts to defend its autonomy against partisan control, and to survive the attacks from socialists and centre parties that refused political recognition to grassroots organizations because they could not claim electoral support' (p. 236). Following the first municipal elections in April 1979, the Citizens' Movement collapsed, unable any longer to sustain the inherent contradiction between its fundamental character as an autonomous social movement and the involvement of mainstream parties in its organisation.

The Citizens' Movement as the archetypal urban social movement

How does Castells himself evaluate the experience of the Citizens' Movement? And on what basis does he feed his conclusions into the model of urban social change and urban social movements?

First of all, he divides the effects achieved by the movement into three categories: the effects on urban service provision and urban development, changes in cultural vitality and nature of community life in the city and, finally, the political effects. These three categories already correspond to his final model of the core elements of an urban social movement which, as we have seen, are collective consumption, community, and political self-management. The methodological problem is whether or not this represents a *post hoc* rationalisation.

Before developing this point the more important question is to determine whether the realities, products and effects achieved by the Citizens' Movement *in fact* measure up to Castells's claims to have discovered a fully fledged urban social movement in the Madrid of the 1970s. He is asking us to believe that the movement achieved, not necessarily on its own but as the primary motorforce, a change of 'urban meaning'.

Undoubtedly the neighbourhood groups achieved some

important policy changes, modifications and innovations in the urban infrastructure and the public services: schools were built, slums demolished and replaced, central Madrid became the subject of a Preservation Authority, and public participation in planning was initiated (although there is no clear evidence whether this was a genuine sharing of policy-making or the screening/legitimising process characteristic of British planning). These were the concrete achievements of the movement, but its extent was limited by economic constraints because the private sector would not in the main co-operate and the public sector was underfunded. As Castells himself says, 'As always, urban change that does not produce *a corresponding social and structural change* is likely to bring on a crisis of some kind' (p. 260, emphasis added). No structural change has apparently occurred.

In the field of 'cultural' developments Castells ascribes two main innovations to the Citizens' Movement. First, the revitalisation of the folk traditions of the city, and second, the growth and strengthening of community life in the neighbourhoods which Castells claims did not exist before the Citizens' Movement: 'In less than five years the city had revived its popular traditions, added new ones and had learnt to express diversity against a background of anonymous bureaucracy and cultural barrenness, *both of which had dominated for forty years*' (p. 260, emphasis added). At the political level the movement was an important focus of popular opposition to the Franquist government, and after Franco's death they were a strong voice in the demand for democratic local elections. It also had the effect of galvanising the political parties into producing programmes that related to the urban issues raised by the neighbourhood organisations. Beyond this it led the Madrid city council to experiment with decentralised community councils: 'Thus the demands for participatory democracy actually reshaped the institutions of city government' (p. 261).

This list of achievements is impressive, but it is very difficult to make the causal connections between what Castells claims and the process of democratisation in post-Franquist Spain. Castells does not claim that the Citizens' Movement alone subverted the fascist dictatorship, but that it was a key instrument in provoking its demise. The movement inserted the range of urban issues into the political arena, rekindled the cultural/folk traditions of the city and was the non-partisan source of demands for a participatory democracy. 'Only when the social groups and a more diversified range of issues, such as the ones posed by the Citizens' Movement, sided against the authoritation state, did the reformist forces within it see the necessity for, and the possibility of, ensuring a peaceful transition to democracy' (p. 263). In the overall urban meaning of the city of Madrid the movement had the specific effect of introducing the notion of 'the city as a use-value'. The basic functions, of capitalist accumulation, bureaucratic power and the symbolic representation of modernisation continued, but were overlain by the popular demand that the city should be 'a collective good, a shared experience and should be governed by its own grassroots' (p. 262).

Castell's assessment is eloquent, but in what sense do these achievements justify the special place of the Citizens' Movement in his new theoretical frame? There are significant problems with the evidence in the book. First, as already suggested, Castells himself says that no structural changes took place in Spanish society as a result of the Citizens' Movement. Madrid, very much in the manner of Glasgow in 1915, became a city in which 'use-value' played a part but there was no question of transforming the core urban meaning away from its capitalist/ bureaucratic past. Most of the important effects described by Castells take place, in fact, at the political level – the Citizens' Movement as a focus of popular opposition to Franquism, as the originator of demands for local democracy in the post-Franquist era, as the object of party political controversies (supported by parties with roots in it, opposed by the main national parties with no electoral linkages as a threat to the party system and politcal order by representing alternative sources of loyalty). Ultimately the weight of these contradictions broke the movement.

This is the crucial problem with Castells's reading of the Citizens' Movement: it had its origins in a unique (in Europe) set of political circumstances (a long-standing, fascist dictatorship). For over forty years political opposition of every variety had been suppressed and the purges of 1969, which generated the Citizens' Movement, represented the oppressive actions of a crumbling régime. Spain was a nation-state linked to a continent of liberal democracies. It can be argued that the key theoretical and model-building lesson of the Madrid movement is in relating the existence and character of urban movements to the party political context of the society (Ceccarelli, 1982; Pickvance, 1983). The key point here, in relation to Spain in the 1970s, is that remarkable as the achievements of the Citizens' Movement might have been, the circumstances of its origins – specifically, the absence of legal opposition political parties – were equally remarkable. Had the starting point for this movement been a liberal democracy rather than a fascist dictatorship, the story would inevitably have been very different. The question remains: is Castells justified in generating his theoretical model of urban social change from a unique history?

A second set of problems surrounds the degree of interpretation Castells has made in his evaluation of the Citizens' Movement. This takes us back to the methodological question raised earlier in the section. To what extent is Castells's model of cross-cultural urban social change a *post hoc* rationalisation? This question links closely to the weight of interpretation Castells puts on his case study. In short, given that the Citizens' Movement is not simply an urban social movement but *the* urban social movement (in the modern period), its characteristics and the effects it achieved need to be firmly grounded. If any one of the core elements cannot be substantiated then, by the terms of Castells's structural model of urban social movements (collective consumption/cultural/political), the movement ceases to be an urban social movement. As Castells argues, 'If the three basic goals are not interconnected in the praxis of the movement, no other element will be able to accomplish a significant change in urban meaning' (p. 323). There needs to be a sufficiently high level of correspondence between the reality and the model for the theoretical/causal links to be sustained. On this basis there are grounds for questioning Castells's prescriptive definitions. A particularly vulnerable part of this case study is his treatment of the cultural effects obtained by the Citizens' Movement. In his specification of the three goals of urban social movements he describes the element of cultural identity in the following terms:

the defense of communication between people, autonomously defined social meaning, and face-to-face interaction, against the monopoly of messages by the media, the predominance of one-way information flows, and the standardization of culture on the basis of increasingly heteronomous sources for the neighbourhood residents. (Castells, 1983, p. 319)

The question is whether this describes what was happening in the Citizens' Movement in Madrid in the 1970s. In his assessment Castells, as we have seen, points to two major effects in this context: (a) 'the most striking effect in this respect was the revitalization of street festivals and popular fairs' (p. 260); and (b) 'the strengthening of local networks and the development of community life' (p. 260). Do these, even supposing they are products only of the Citizens' Movement, amount to a sufficient level of effect to be claimed as one of the core themes of an archetypal urban social movement?

Here we must discuss a further problem in this text, namely Castells's re-introduction of the notion of 'community' which he dismissed so scathingly as ideological in his early works. It is one of the most difficult and controversial concepts in modern sociology, ranking only with the notion of class in this respect. As shown in Chapter 1, Castells formerly related the theory of community to the ideological genesis of 'urbanism; but in his 1983 text, he seems to have forgotten about this issue. He himself says of the Citizens' Movement that it 'generally reacted negatively to the disruption of traditional ways of life, particularly family life and patriarchal authority' (p. 271). It was, he admits, 'culturally conservative'. But all of this is overridden by Castells because the movement triggered what he calls 'community building'. What Castells means by this is unclear. He refers to the substitution of 'communication for loneliness, solidarity for aggressiveness, and local customs for mass media's monopoly of the message' (p. 271). Whatever he means, there is a tautology because he goes on to suggest that this process of community building was limited by people's conventional attitudes – hence the dominant cultural community embraced by the Madrid Citizens' Movement was not the women's movement, the youth movement or any of the radical alternatives, but family life: 'the lowest common denominator was generally adopted, and challenges and experimentation were not welcome' (p. 271). Once again we must query whether, in the context of virtually every other Western nation at the time, the contribution of the Citizens' Movement can be considered as a seminal experience. Castells claims that 'The search for community was the one truly original, fundamental, cultural dimension of Madrid's Citizens' Movement' (p. 272). Even accepting the analytical/definitional problems of the concept of community, in what sense was the movement an innovatory force in its cultural mode? The difficulty is that if Castells, as he does, sees the Madrid experience as the foundation of a cross-cultural, comparative theory of urban social movements, the example he has taken is not particularly exceptional in the European context but may be innovatory in the Spanish context. The Madrid Citizens' Movement was leading from behind.

Having established the Madrid movement as the model, archetypal urban social movement, Castells then goes on to judge all other urban movements by the Madrid yardstick. For example, he defines the protest groups in the Parisian Grandes Ensembles as 'collective consumption trade unions', that is to say (in the French context) that because the Labour and trade union movements failed to take up the issues of the social wage and the urban services, the missing level of representation was self-generated in the areas themselves. The organisations that were generated, however, did not move out of the 'trade union' dimension (the demand for services) into the wider cultural and political spheres. They did not move into the political arena, Castells argues, because of the support for the election of left-wing municipal governments. As Castells says, 'Thus it (the Grandes Ensembles movement) obtained urban demands but disappeared as a movement when a left-wing municipality was elected' (Castells, 1983, p. 323). But was not this exactly what happened to the Madrid Citizens' Movement? Having been party to the overthrow of Franquism and the restoration of democracy, the impact of the first municipal elections in Madrid – with the return of a left-wing council – was the total collapse of the movement. It was the same effect for the same reason. Once again the crucial factor was the possible (and then actual) existence of Left parties committed to programmes or urban reform and drawing support from the urban movements. Having succeeded to power they become the main instrument for progressing urban demands. This pattern is repeated in parts of Britain.

Using the experience of the Madrid Citizens' Movement, Castells has elaborated a structural model for the definition of urban social movements. To repeat: they must articulate the three goals of collective consumption, community culture and political self-management; they must be aware of their role as an urban social movement; they must 'connect' to the media, professionals and political parties; and finally, they must be politically autonomous of any party. By this model every other urban movement everywhere in the globe is to be judged. Some lack one thing, some lack another, and accordingly they can be labelled. This method is a replication of his phase one theory of urban social movements, except in that case the criteria were different. Then the essential point was whether an urban movement was linked into the advanced working-class movement. If it was it became an urban social movement, and so capable of achieving structural changes; otherwise movements were graded according to whether they were reformist or participatory, and in either case were assumed not to be capable of activating sustained effects on the social structure. With the 1983 model we are invited to undertake the same process of screening. What has changed are the criteria for making our judgements. But Castells's new formula is as unsound as his previous one (Pickvance, 1976; Saunders, 1979; also refer to the first part of this chapter). There are strong grounds for doubting whether the Madrid Citizens' Movement can be considered the archetypal urban social movement, first, because the historical circumstances of Spain in the late 1960s and 1970s were exceptional in the context of Western politics as a whole, and second, because the empirical evidence is not sufficently weighty to sustain a 'cross-cultural' model of urban social change. The cultural horizons of the movement were conservative, and it is doubtful whether it did *in practice* achieve a meaningful degree of political self-management before collapsing in the wake of the 1979 local elections.

Finally, these empirical inconsistencies and interpretative problems may not have seemed important to Castells. If the aim was to achieve a structural model of urban social change from the outset, then it seems likely that whatever evidence was found a model could be produced. There is a strong element of *post hoc* rationalisation in Castells's thinking.

Conclusion

The manner in which Castells defines and uses the notion of urban social movements has passed through three major phases. In phase one the emphasis was on the role of urban social movements in linking secondary structural contradictions in the urban system into the anti-capitalist struggle, centred on the advanced sections of the working-class movement. This position was subject to a number of criticisms, notably by Pickvance, who argued that the notion that *only* urban social movements can create system change or adaptations of policy ignores the possibility that purely institutional sources may lead to change.

> there seems no justification for going to the extreme of saying that urban social movements are the exclusive source of (small) changes. On the one hand such a view ignores the pressures exerted by other urban actors (e.g. land-owners, financial institutions) and on the other hand it fails to recognize that local authorities may have their own policy preferences which results from the clash between departments (and groups of professionals) local-central conflicts, the goals of the controlling political party, etc. (Pickvance, 1976a, p. 207)

Dunleavy points out that if factors internal to the state can create small changes, then it follows that large-scale change arising from the same source is also possible. By the same token, if Pickvance had cited examples that involved more radical and highly mobilised urban movements, then movement-instigated change would seem a more viable proposition. Indeed, he acknowledges the point.

> My aim is not to deny that mobilization is an important source of social change, indeed I would suspect that the larger the change the more important it would be. (Pickvance, 1976a, p. 211)

Having determined that protest movements are not the exclusive source of change, the empirical analysis of the methods deployed by the state apparatus to exert its influence on events becomes a fundamental area of study. This in fact leads to an important neo-elitist literature, largely ignored by Castells, which demonstrates the range of strategies and resources that are potentially available for deployment against protest movements. Dunleavy, for example, illustrates many of these points in his study of the high-rise housing boom in which tenants and other potential clients for this type of housing were effectively blocked from influencing the decision process, even in the wake of the Ronan Points disaster (Dunleavy, 1977). Lukes (1975), in the most important discussion in this area, argues that political power has an invisible face that operates through social processes and structures to limit and suppress conflict. The investigations of all forms of urban protest potentially unlocks for analysis whole areas of hidden and latent conflict together with the processes and structural interests that operate to contain and limit conflict. Several of the case studies in later chapters illustrate some of the strategies and resources that are ranged against urban movements. To some extent Castells responds to this area of critcism in his second-phase material in which, it will be recalled, an important development is his identification of sectoral consumption cleavages that are not determined by class action, but by people's position within the consumption process itself. Once he concedes that the class/ structure axis is not exclusively determinant in the social process, the way is clear, indeed it becomes a necessity, to explain how consumption cleavages operate and to what political effect. Here Castells makes an important distinction between public and private distribution and provision of consumption services and draws particular attention to the selection process used by the authorities to determine the access of groups and individuals. For example, in housing the private sector institutions are particularly concerned with a client's creditworthiness, in the public sector the housing administrators tend to marginalise minorities – blacks, youth, single parents – while 'the ability to manoeuvre inside the bureaucratic network of public assistance in order to win one's case is a socially determined cultural acquisition' (Castells, 1978a, p. 23).

Having accepted a managerialist influence in decision-making, Castells reasserts the role of urban social movements as the major element in urban-based social change and links the existence of consumption cleavages to the broadening of the anti-capitalist struggle via cross-class alliances. He does not, at this stage, pick up on the thrust of the neo-elitist argument and only partially answers Pickvance's critique (of the institutional source of small-scale change). By drawing out the crucial interrelationship between the public and private provision of collective consumption in the context of the dominant private sector, Castells has pointed to a major analytical element in urban political analysis (explored notably by Dunleavy, 1980 and 1983).

A second important area of criticism of Castells's phase one position concerns the way in which urban social movements are generated and how they achieve 'effects' on the social system. As we have seen, his thesis (at least until the mid-1970s) hinged on the presence of a political cadre capable of linking urban issues into the advanced working-class movement. 'The role of the organisation . . . is fundamental', writes Castells in *The Urban Question*. The problem here, as Pickvance points out, is that the implementation of a revolutionary political organisation into urban protest movements is an inadequate explanation of how a social movement develops (or equally, in the light of the earlier point, does not develop). Neither does it explain the conditions under which a particular social base and issue will be receptive to an outside political influence, nor that there may be tactical avenues available to groups as a result of internal contacts with the authorities or from links into the wider community. 'This is true irrespective of whether the underlying theory of political action stresses mobilization of the base, institutional means, or personal relations' (Pickvance, 1976b, p. 218).

It is clearly the case that unless in every case where the key elements in Castells's formulation are present (issue, social base, political organisation) and the situation does not respond according to the urban social movements model, then some other, or at the very least, some additional, causal factors must be at work. As Saunders suggest, there is a basic flaw in Castells's proposition in trying to relate contradictions to the achievement of certain types of effect through the mediation of political struggle because Castells' ends up by arguing that class struggle arises as a result of system contradiction, but while he can theorise the latter he has no way of linking them to the former' (Saunders, 1981, p. 202).

Furthermore, the argument that urban social movements are frequently 'pluriclass' in their nature is also an improbable political scenario because consumption issues may in fact be highly *divisive*, not only separating, say, middle-class owner occupiers from working-class council tenants (Saunders, 1979), but by dividing the workers among themselves – in this instance manual worker home-owners and non-home-owners (given that approximately 50 per cent of manual workers are owner occupiers). This type of argument is the basis of what Pickvance calls 'the urban fallacy' – that a consumption interest does not necessarily lead to the supersession of traditional class divisions. But in his 'middle' phase Castells does recognise that consumption cleavages may produce autonomous political organisation not necessarily linked to a vanguard party for the production of 'effects'. This position arises from his upgrading of the urban process within his theoretical perspective and also from the adoption of a Eurocommunist outlook with an emphasis on building a popular front. Here the linkage of the classes occurs not only in the medium of urban social movements but in a broadly based alliance of organisations with a variety of social class bases all ranged against the dominance of capital. Consumption issues do then provide a significant contribution to the inter-class political struggle (composed of the workers' movement, movements of professionals and 'the salaried classes', the ecologists and others).

As a result of the emphasis in both phase one and phase two on the role of political organisation in the mobilisation process, Castells failed to explore sociologically a theme that he now regards as central to his analysis, that of the definition of social bases, i.e. the constituency of people who make up the potential source of an urban movement. When Castells does discuss this theme in his earlier texts (for example, in his case study of the Pobladores squatter camps in Chile), the emphasis is almost entirely on the class composition of the camps and the type of political 'line' that develops as a result. Any suggestion of subjectivity, of how people feel and are motivated to act, is consistently denied by Castells:

For who are these 'actors'? Can they be defined in themselves without reference to the social context they express? . . . But in the end one is dealing with men it will be said. Yes, but apprehended in what way? As 'citizens' or as members of a social class or class section? In which of their different roles? Placed in what social contradiction? Subjected to what ideological communication? Engaged in what political process? (Castells, 1977, p. 251)

But in *The City and the Grassroots* Castells discovers the realm of 'personal experience' as a crucial factor in any 'meaningful structure of historical action':

Collective action is usually seen as a reaction to a crisis created by an economically determined structural logic . . . As a result we are left with urban systems separated from personal experience; with structures without actors, and actors without structures; with cities without citizens and citizens without cities . . . This book, on the contrary, assumes that only by analysing the relationship between people and urbanization will be able to understand cities and citizens at the same time. (Castells, 1983, p. xvi)

Having responded to the criticisms of Pickvance, Rex and others, we argue that Castells has still not integrated a sociological understanding of the importance of the nature and characteristics of social bases in the mobilisation process; of how a social base becomes, or fails to become, a social force. What Castells has done, and this is important, is to draw attention to the significance of local communities as focal points of urban movement activity. As he argues at the end of *The City and the Grassroots*, in the face of the overwhelming national and international sources of political power, 'people go home. Most withdraw individually, but the crucial, active minority, anxious to retaliate, organize themselves on their local turf' (1983, p. 330). He goes on to suggest it is here that new social movements, which may form the basis of future societies, are nurtured. It certainly is the case in Britain that the neighbourhood level and residential community have been and remain major social bases of urban movement activity. This is discussed in some detail in the next chapter.

One other important innovation in Castells's social/cultural analysis of urban social change is the recognition he now gives to the role of women. In his earlier texts Castells paid only scant attention to the theme of feminism and the politics of gender. But throughout *The City and the Grassroots* women are described as having a special place in urban struggles. For example, he describes the Glasgow Rent Strike of 1915 as 'a women's movement that fell short of being a feminist movement' (1983, p. 33). In the historical case studies women are seen as mobilising on behalf of their "families' needs" in the context of the evolution of urban-based class and power struggles. It is not made entirely clear why women carry this special range of functions or the terms of the relationship between women's struggles and the feminist movement. Castells argues that the feminist consciousness is about 'overcoming the structural domination of one gender by another' (p. 309), but in the urban experience of social change suggests that

> The redifinition of urban meaning to emphasise use value and the quality of experience over exchange value and centraliza- tion of management is historically connected to the feminist theme of identity and communication. (Castells, 1983, p. 309)

The problem here is that although Castells sees the feminist movement as a key battleground in the liberation struggles it is not theorised into his model. The position is equivalent to his ambiguous treatment of political parties, the media and the professions: they are seen as 'connected' to urban social change but must not impinge on the autonomy of urban social movements to innovate new meaning systems. The women's movement stands in much the same sort of relationship. We are given no insight into why the themes of 'identity' or 'commun- ication' are specifically women's issues, or into the nature of the connection to social change and his specification of urban social movements.

Criticisms of other aspects of *The City and the Grassroots* (phase three) were made in the last section: his use of history in structuring his new theoretical model; questions about the validity of his empirical findings and methodology; his failure to theorise the feminist theme; the strategy problem, or urban social movements being reliant on other bodies to carry through structural social change; and the question of whether Castells's cross-cultural theory of urban social change is an adequate comparative model for explaining the global experience of urban social movements.

Some of these criticisms are integral to our own understanding of urban social movements in the political system. In Chapter 3 we outline a range of core themes, built around the critique of Castells's work in this chapter, which provide the framework for the case-study presentations in Chapters 4, 5 and 6.

Chapter 3

The Mobilisation Process

This chapter focuses on key elements which underpin the creation of urban movement activity and sustain their involvements, or, by the same token, inhibit the mobilisation process. Mobilisation is taken to mean, therefore, both organisational action and also non-protest on apparently objective issue bases. Action and non-action need to be held within the same analytical framework (Dunleavy, 1977). This chapter draws on themes that are found in Castells's material but which he does not fully explore. In the British context these are the political structure and processes of local political systems, the identification of social bases and their potential to generate urban movements, and the pervasive influence of a range of key urban system ideologies which directly condition the genesis of some groups and underlie the whole of the local political system.

The use of a thematic approach enables a more open-ended discussion than the tightly structured models suggested by Castells. In a relatively immature field of analysis, modelling methodologies potentially conceal as much as they illuminate because the tendency is to concentrate on the internal logic and coherence of the model. This issue crops up again in Chapter 6, where Castells's cross-cultural comparative model is discussed along with a comparative model for understanding urban social movements recently proposed by Pickvance (1983).

The local political system

Castells's analytical perspective, although aware of the institutional constraints, and increasingly seeing this level as harbouring political power, embraces a relatively narrow spectrum of political processes. It is argued here that a core determinant of the character, strategies and impact of urban social movements in Britain is the special nature of the local political system (Dearlove, 1973; Saunders, 1979; Dunleavy, 1980).

There are three main components in this analysis, although the three areas overlap in many respects. First, the existence of many urban protest organisations arises from a formal political system that is generally insulated from effective influence by the public and is oligarchic in its pattern of control. Issue groups emerge because formal political channels offer little scope for effecting changes of policy direction. Second, the dominance of the local authorities in local politics, with important areas of autonomy from central government, is a strong influence on the tactics adopted by non-party groups, which also feeds into the organisational types. Third, there is evidence of an osmosis of individual actors and even groups of activists from local campaigns into the party political system underscoring and in some cases causing power struggles, particularly in the process of the generational succession of party notables and leaders.

The single most important factor about local government in this context is the broadly two-party division of influence in the political control of local councils. This has been a characteristic of British politics for over half a century, despite evidence of a strong tradition of independents (Grant, 1977) and is particularly a feature of the reorganised post-1974 system. Furthermore, control of many councils does not oscillate between the competing parties but tends to remain in almost permanent control of one or other party. Many rural areas have been in Conservative contol (or of Conservative-inclined independents) for generations. Conversely, many of the inner London boroughs and boroughs in the towns and cities in the North of England have been controlled by Labour for decades; in some cases since the mid-1920s. Dunleavy estimates that in the post-1974 reorganised local government system 75 per cent of the population of England and Wales live in areas where one-party control of the most important tier of local government may be expected to be continuous. The important point here is that the notion of an electorally responsive local government system is significantly tarnished. As Dunleavy observes, 'local council groups can pursue virtually any policy without worrying at all about losing elections' (Dunleavy, 1980, p. 138).

Britain has not, therefore, undergone the transference of power experienced in many Continental countries in the late 1970s, anticipated, according to Ceccarelli (1982), by the activity of urban social movements. This relatively stable and long-term political control of large areas of local government exerts an important influence on the character and strategies of urban protest organisations in Britain compared to the Continent. The dominance of the orthodoxy of electoral responsiveness and accountability is also a powerful influence on the tactical stance adopted by 'outsider' groups. (This process will be discussed more fully in the section on the ideologies of local politics.) The limited evidence that exists indicates that groups with different political goals receive differential access to the local political system according to the political complexion of the ruling party. The standard evidence on this is found in Dearlove's account of the Conservative-controlled London Borough of Kensington and Chelsea. Here the councillors effectively vetted outside pressure groups and other organisations according to whether they were broadly in sympathy with local policy or against it. On this criterion groups were labelled as 'helpful' or 'unhelpful' and their degree of access controlled accordingly. There are grounds for considering this an over-restricted model because marginalised groups may extort concessions from the local authority by other means – in the case of council house tenants, for example, by the use of rent strikes – and the balance of power in central/local government relations may modify the terms on which groups become acceptable or not. For example, with central government currently restricting the flow of funds into local services and attempting to abolish the metropolitan counties, campaigns that link a wide spectrum of local organisations, trade unions and political representatives and party groups are commonplace. But the pattern of one-party control of local government generally does impose a limited range of strategies on groups seeking policy change of some sort (Lowe, 1977). In Britain the very strong tendency for groups in this position is either to develop by various means a bargaining relationship with the local authority, often short-circuiting the political members and approaching directly the departmental level, or to cultivate 'insider' contacts, political and/or executive, as the most likely means of initiating policy changes or procedural and administrative amendments. Writing about some 4700 voluntary organisations identified in Birmingham in the mid-1970s, Newton observes, 'time and time again the interviews showed a series of elaborate networks of quasi-official and semi-official communications linking community organisations and local government departments' (Newton, 1976, p. 66). However, most of the groups in Newton's study were well-established and uncontroversial bodies with few overt political ambitions. They were mainly sports clubs, youth groups or church organisations that posed no threat to mainstream council policy. Urban social movements are not directly discussed by Newton, although some of his sample do fall within the broadly based definition used in this text. By their very nature, with groups whose existence is sometimes transient or sporadic, insider connections are unlikely to be as strong in processing their grievances compared with conventional voluntary associations or pressure groups. Most of these organisations exist as a result of opposition to some aspect of local policy. Issues that develop around urban policy – opposition to slum-clearance schemes, to rent or rate increases, to road extensions or widening, or to school closures – often provoke non-party protest movements simply because access through conventional or insider networks is difficult to effect. The existence of these issues implies degrees of criticism of local policy or administrative practice and the groups inevitably come to be classified as 'unhelpful'. Urban social movements must, therefore, decide how to progress their campaigns, either by direct action or by establishing the basis of a negotiating position with the authority. Both methods are fraught with problems but both can and have succeeded, although often leading to unintended consequences. The strategy problems of urban protest groups are discussed in later chapters.

Although the tendency is to label groups according to the extent of their challenge in the policy arena, it is also the case that local authorities in Britain have themselves sought to develop limited forms of 'community' involvement in some areas of service provision. This partly derives from statutory obligations in town planning and housing legislation. But these exercises in 'public participation' are primarily intended to enhance the one-way flow of information from the planners to citizens and are perhaps best understood as a means of legitimating a closed planning process. The monitoring of group activities also serves to provide early warning of public disquiet over particular issues. As Dunleavy argues,

> Interest groups have been widely embraced as a means of screening out of the political and administrative process the potential overload of individual citizens' grievances and views. (Dunleavy, 1980, p. 184)

The growth of urban social movements outside the formalised political system has not been contained by these institutional initiatives. Tenants' associations, redevelopment action groups, hospital defence committees, squatters' associations, ratepayers' associations have all become or been important focal points of urban change and conflict. They are, however, constrained by the dominance of the local authority in local politics which is a ready-made policy-making area. At the same time the inaccessibility of the formal party political system generates the conditions under which urban social movements develop.

Some activists from the grassroots organisations penetrated the party systems either as a long-term tactic of influencing policy in specific areas or on a more generalised basis. The agenda and the actors within local parties are influenced in a fairly systematic way by an osmosis of individuals from urban protest organisations into the party system. Although the evidence for this is limited, it would seem to be more common in Labour-controlled authorities because these tend to be the city areas with a wider range of public services than elsewhere, and the ambience of the local political system may be more open. For some people involvement in a local issue is a politicising experience leading them to join a party. Labour has a more open party organisation, although membership is to some extent screened by the constitutency parties. In some cases activists are encouraged to join the local party as a means to the incorporation of a protest movement that might be electorally threatening (Sklair, 1975). The Liberals also attract community activists; especially in areas dominated by right-wing Labour councillors (where local Labour Parties are often very weak), the platform of 'community politics' is an attractive alternative and has achieved some notable electoral successes. Examples of this process of 'drift' from urban protest organisations into the party political system are described in Chapters 4 and 5.

But a major determinant of the character of urban social movements in the British context is the strong tendency, as we have seen, towards long-term, one-party, political control of local government. Many groups are formed in response to the difficulties of fighting an issue through the formal party system, but the 'town hall' is inevitably regarded as the major store of political power. The tactics and strategy of non-party movements are consequently invariably directed towards establishing some form of negotiating position with the relevant service departments. Direct action in the form of rent or rate strikes is a tactic of last resort and often the hope is that the threat of such action is sufficient in itself to achieve policy changes. Violent confrontation is rare and certainly does not occur systematically or on a calculated spectrum of effectiveness as appeared to be the case in the United States in the 1960s and 1970s (Friedland, 1982). In Britain violent action is usually politically counter-productive. The important point is that urban social movements in this country, because of the structure and political/ideological context of local government, are less visible than elsewhere, but this should not be read as lack of vitality. It is a tactical response to a certain set of historical and institutional realities. Castells's method does not take into account the specific nature of local political systems and, as a result, fails to pinpoint a main influence on urban social movement development and types.

Social bases and the mobilisation process

Another theme which Castells does not fully explore, although his work contains important innovative thinking on it, is the nature and characteristics of the social bases around which collective action might or might not be generated. His identification of consumption cleavages which have an independent existence in the social system (a 'middle phase' finding) is very significant in this context. But there are consistent and major omissions in this theme, particularly his failure to theorise non-action and the absence of any discussion of the sociology of social base structure and formation, of how people subjectively understand and act on issues of common concern. In *The City and the Grassroots*, Castells does belatedly embrace the whole realm of 'personal experience' as a centrepiece of the urban system, but he still does not analytically incorporate the sociological relevance of social process into his method.

This section addresses this most important subject area, and is located again in a British context, to show how the experience of one country has been shaped and developed. It is at the level of single nations that the application of Castells's cross-cultural model falters because it lacks empirical grounding.

Under what circumstances are British citizens as residents and consumers of public services motivated to take collective action? By the same token, what factors have inhibited urban communities from responding to the large and small-scale changes constantly wrought on the built environment and the urban public services by politicians, planners and business enterprises in the last two decades? The question of how a 'social base' becomes a 'social force' (Olives, 1976) has only been discussed in the restricted context of some neo-Marxist literature. The question of political inertia and non-protest is virtually unexplored, yet in theoretical terms it holds a number of keys to the development of our knowledge about political systems and processes (Dunleavy, 1977). Most studies of local politics and pressure groups start at the point where the organisation already exists and assume a relationship between groups and their constituencies and members. This approach misses some vital lessons about the genesis of movements, the institutional definition of issues in the urban environment, and the routes by which social and economic stakes are embraced and metamorphosed by the formal administrative/political system.

This section examines evidence on these themes from a variety of sources, mainly from urban sociology, and identifies the existence of networks of associational activity within local social systems. It is assumed that any form of collective action is predicated by different modes and patterns of organisation within the social system that will either need to be harnessed or in some way overcome if a new associational form is to develop. Useful evidence on this is to be found in the ageing 'community studies' from the 1950s and in the work of Rex and Moore

(1967) and Rex (1973). Other writers show that the notion of 'community' can best be defined as a base on which social movements form, but that these divisions are the creation of governmental agencies concerned to segment urban areas into convenient and controllable units (Janowitz, 1952; Suttles, 1972). More recently developments from Castells's 'middle phase' work has led to a redefinition of the contents of the urban system which is centred on a series of sectoral consumption bases (Castells, 1978a; Dunleavy, 1979, 1983). This section is drawn, therefore, from work spanning four decades from a wide spectrum of theoretical schools.

The social bases on which collective action most frequently develops in the urban social system are (a) residential communities and (b) a variety of sectoral consumption cleavages (Dunleavy, 1980), but the distinction between these types of base is not always clear and often they will merge, most obviously in the housing sphere itself. For example, council house tenants are often a rigidly demarcated geographical community but they also share a common consumption interest (public sector housing). Residential communities are defined by a mix of socially determined boundaries and the 'districting' of external agencies. Consumption cleavages that cross-cut the general social structure are defined by shared access to a publicly or privately consumed service. It does not follow, of course, that urban social movements necessarily develop from these bases but they do have the greatest objective potential for a collective response because there are distinct material interests at stake, and are frequently the targets of the policy process.

The community studies

Although it is now accepted that the notion of 'community' as an autonomous social system is a sociological ideal type with little analytical value, the 1950s and early 1960s saw the production of large numbers of 'community studies' based on this view. Although people do see their lives in limited spatial 'home areas' (Hampton, 1970) with networks of associational activity, to restrict an analysis of the origins of urban protest to this parochial sphere would be misleading. It is, however, a backcloth against which some of the processes involved in mobilisation must be read, and it is within the community studies that evidence of social process in residential areas can be gleaned. This section makes critical and qualified use of these studies because much of the community studies literature is dated, and patterns of social life have evolved rapidly since the 1950s and 1960s. But they do highlight the practical significance of the sociology of community for urban movement development. Moreover, as indicated in Chapter 2, Castells himself now looks to the face-to-face level of the social system as a major source of social movement activity; indeed, his current political perspective is highly dependent on the notion of community as a home area (as we shall see more fully in Chapter 7). While not necessarily wrong, the argument here is that the sociological analysis of community points to the parochial and limiting nature of this social level and creates the possibility of barriers to solidarity as well as being a generating mechanism of some types of social base.

The most fruitful phase for the English community studies was occurring when the influence of the 'Chicago School' of urban sociologists, dating from the pre-1939 decades, was still potent. In the seminal work of Burgess, McKenzie and Park, urban communities are seen as ecologically distinct units with internally coherent systems of social relations – 'a mosaic of little worlds which touch but do not interpenetrate'. For their part, the British community studies had a particular fascination with the empirical analysis of 'working-class communities' which were thought of as harbouring a distinctive subculture characterised by solidaristic and closely knit social systems. With the exception of Bell's study of families in Swansea (Bell, 1969), there seemed to be no corresponding idea of 'middle-class' community, which, when it did appear, was in the context of a suburbanisation thesis or of the effects of commuting, both bringing the middle classes into contact with predominantly working-class social milieux (Pahl, 1970) or vice versa (Wilmott and Young, 1970).

This concentration of research effort reflected the social reality of a diversity of types of working-class community in the 1950s. The post-war spread of home and car ownership into the manual worker strata has, however, created distinct consumption interests across the class spectrum which blur the boundaries between the early representations of community. The existence of working-class community and the growth of cross-cutting consumption factors, may be usefully understood in terms of Parkin's notion of 'dominant' and 'subordinate' value systems (Parkin, 1971). Here a contrast is drawn between nationally created value for legitimising the social system and an essentially parochial subordinate value system typified by the archetypal working-class community, 'representing a design for living based upon localised social knowledge and face-to-face relationships'. Working-class communities develop their own patterns of life and distinctive qualities because there is no universal subordinate value system. Middle-class residential communities are located in the dominant system of values and are characterised by their adherence to property ownership, occupational security and nationally structured professions. Consumption divisions, particularly the changing sectoral balance in housing and transport, have extended the dominant value system into the manual worker population. The significance of this for urban social movements is discussed in the next section.

But important residual features of traditional working-class life remain and continue to provide identifiable social bases with distinctive social mechanisms for evolving or inhibiting the evaluation of associational activity. This is why the ageing community studies are still of interest because they contain a wealth of information about locally based associational behaviour. How do residential social bases, in the confines of the subordinate value system, organise themselves? Read as a group of studies, one thing is very clear: that different experiences of community create different patterns of public organisational activity. At a practical level, one of the main problems facing new local movements is precisely how to penetrate or harness established networks of associational activity, which are often informal and relatively unstructured. The informal nature of working-class organisation in the community is illustrated in Broady's study of Coronation street parties. In a traditional working-class community in Birkenhead, Broady describes how an informal network, built on neighbourliness and years of shared experiences and common adversity, emerged spontaneously to organise the street celebrations. Broady points to the strong tradition of informal co-operation in 'respectable' working-class communities. Normally the mechanisms operate under conditions of adversity, but the same network can respond to other activities. In a West Riding mining village the same instrumental attitude to associational activity was apparent (Dennis, Henriques and Slaughter, 1956). But in this case the network was strongly influenced by the male-dominated trade union. The union is influential beyond the workplace and can invoke a strong sense of union loyalty, which appeared to be synonymous with support for the village community, to impose its decisions.

Working-class community is characterised by an instrumental attitude towards public organisation. Whether in the female-centred tradition of neighbourly co-operation or in the male trade union-dominated mining villages, organisation outside the family fulfils specific needs. People are not drawn into wider co-operation without compelling reasons, and normally the first response is to look towards the established local networks. Similar findings can be found in studies of council house estates, particularly in the early stages of community formation on new estates (Durant, 1939; Lupton and Mitchell, 1954; Hodges and Smith, 1954). The early formation of a tenants' association is characteristic of the initial moving-in phase – to counteract the hostility of nearby private residents, or to deal with complaints about the estate, and generally as a means for facilitating social contact. Later these associations change their functions or disintegrate as the local networks become established and the socialisation function gives way to more specialised organisations.

One important feature of all the community studies is the pattern of status differentiation that pervades working-class communities as they were portrayed in the 1950s and 1960s. People regarded themselves as 'respectable', keeping themselves to themselves, compared to residents in nearby streets, or differentiated between people being at the 'top end' compared to those at the 'bottom end' of an estate. Not only does this influence patterns of associational behaviour, but it strongly supports the idea that working-class community is mainly confined to localised face-to-face relationships. The subordinate value system is characterised by its accommodation to the everyday experiences of working-class life. Local associational behaviour in working-class communities may be antipathetic to wider political class consciousness (Runicman, 1966; Westergaard, 1965), but this conclusion needs to be modified in the light of more recent evidence about the processes of associational activity. This issue will be discussed later in the chapter. Here the concern is to introduce the mechanisms of associational behaviour in different types of traditional community, and to suggest that a precise knowledge of the social histories and social structures of individual areas is a prerequisite to understanding how and under what circumstances the mobilisation process operates.

The pattern of social life, demography and social structure in the 1980s have changed dramatically over the last twenty years. To focus only on traditional working-class community would be misleading. Families are smaller, there are a million single-parent households, most women work, a high proportion of working-class families own their own houses and often a car (a majority of skilled manual workers are owner occupiers), and slum clearance has dispersed many of the old communities. One further major change has been the growth of the urban public services, subsidised and provided by the state. The growth of consumption-based sectoral divisions, which cut across the conventional social class system, are important as a new source of social bases, although the distinctions between residential community and consumption-based divisions is not always clear-cut.

Sectoral consumption cleavages as social bases

As shown in Chapter 1, Castells's recognition of distinct 'consumption cleavages' had major consequences for his political perspective and the general evolution of his reading of the urban system and process. This was a 'phase two' finding and makes an important break with his earlier structuralist neo-Marxism. He described what were effectively autonomous material interests, based on the public or private access to consumption provision, that cut across the social class system and were the source of 'pluriclass' alliances (and were able, therefore, to feed into his Eurocommunist 'popular front' political perspective). But the formation of inter-class movements do not necessarily follow from the growth of consumption cleavages (Saunders, 1979) because they sustain distinct material interests leading to potentially conflictive situations.

This identification and detailed specification of sectoral consumption divisions in the social system is particularly associated with the work in the last five years of Dunleavy. The contents of the consumption field as Dunleavy defines it will be reviewed, including a recent modification to his position, in which emphasis is placed on socialised consumption as a strategy for combating the long-term crisis of under-consumption in advanced capitalist economies. However, it is in the distinct interests built on sectoral access to urban public services that social base formation has occurred: for example, the division between home owners and council tenants, or between private education and state schooling. Dunleavy argues that sectoral consumption cleavages are a major social system development and are a consequence of the rapid post-war expansion of the consumption services. In his first approach to this Dunleavy was concerned to elaborate Castells's notion of collective consumption by identifying precisely which services and policy areas constituted the 'urban' sytem. In answer to this he produced a screened list of services on the basis of their mode of provision (collective or individual) within the public or private sector and/or whether access to it is granted on market or non-market criteria. In this way services such as gas and electricity supply or telephones are excluded because, although they are provided by a public corporation, they are marketed on the basis of individual payments and are commercially funded (Dunleavy, 1980, p. 53). But a facility such as public sector housing is included in the urban field because it is allocated on non-market criteria of need, despite being managed on a quasi-commercial basis with substantial payments made by the consumers. The degree of social cleavage, and its political and ideological significance, created by these sectoral allocation processes is largely dependent on whether a particular service is predominantly provided in the public or private sector. Dunleavy follows Castells in identifying housing and transport as major and distinct consumption items because provision is more evenly split between the sectors than in other services; in Britain, for example, there is a relatively small private sector in education and most people look to the state as the principal provider of this service, but in housing the private sector commands two-thirds of the market, with the remaining third in the public sector. A key point here is that the social composition of housing tenures does not correspond with the social class system; that is to say, 50 per cent of manual workers are owner occupiers. The consumption cleavage in housing is therefore more pronounced among the manual worker strata (with a 50/50 divide on ownership and renting) than other sections of the population. Where the balance of sectoral provision is more heavily weighted to either the public or the private sector, cleavages are less marked. However, private education and private health care – both small-scale providers – offer examples of important bases of ideological structuring and political conflict 'disproportionate in terms of its relevance for the mass of people' (Dunleavy, 1980, p. 81). In other words, sectoral cleavages can generate an impact, politically and ideologically, even when the balance of provision is heavily skewed towards a dominant sector.

Dunleavy sees the major repercussion of consumption cleavages in their effect on conventional explanations of political party alignments among the electorate. There is a strong tendency for Labour and the Conservatives to represent respectively the public and private service divide, generally implying a fragmentation of the Labour vote because major consumption interests cut across the manual worker population more sharply than the non-manual grades. This factor is particularly potent in housing where, as previously argued, owner occupancy (ideologically aligned to the Conservatives) has spread to a high, and increasing, proportion of manual workers. But the evidence for this pattern of alignment based on sectoral divisions awaits systematic testing.

In his more recent work Dunleavy changes the thrust of his analysis by collapsing the public/private distinctions into the exchange processes involved in socialised consumption. His new position argues that the general profile of expenditure on welfare and public service provision is upwards. He focuses in particular on the role of urban interventions in the economic development of market societies, especially in combating the tendency in advanced capitalist economies for an over-production/under-consumption crisis (Baran and Sweezy, 1968). He argues that the massive switch of resources and social organisation towards socialised consumption in this century should be read as one of three major strategies for coping with under-consumption. The other two are, first, the lengthening of production chains (involving an expansion of intermediate production processes and tertiary services, with no increase in final output), and second, spending on defence (much of which is never consumed and is occasionally destroyed in combat) and on advanced technology. Both of these are limited as options due to factors such as population size and the loss of production to overseas competitors, but socialised consumption is a more 'widely available strategy for combating under-consumption tendencies'.

Dunleavy argues that there are two characteristics of socialised consumption that assist its role in extending the range of 'unmet wants'. First, many of the major services within the socialised consumption process are compulsory, giving citizens no choice whether or not to participate. Examples of compulsory consumption are the education of children between 5 and 16 years old, social services regulation over family life, many aspects of the urban planning system, the police and fire services. As a 'deviant' form of consumption in market economies, compulsory socialised consumption services create a unique, non-market linking between government and society. Compulsory consumption may be seen as a provider of welfare, a form of social control and as the basis for extending the range of services largely insulated from citizen accountability, in which new resources and markets can be generated (complementary consumption).

The second aspect of socialised consumption that gives it a strategic place in combating economic under-consumption results from the 'coerced exchange' character of many of the involvements (Mishan, 1967). Here it is argued that for people to avoid a deterioration in their standard of welfare they are compelled to switch from reliance on a public service to a marketed form of provision. For example, in urban transport, as the use of cars progressively becomes the dominant mode of transport, and as a consequence the public transit networks deteriorate through underuse, more and more people need to become car-owners to sustain their mobility. Although initiated by purely market preference by wealthy people for individual-ised transport, less affluent people are gradually forced into a coerced exchange as car ownership develops.

> Large scale 'exiting' from one mode of consuming a product or from one sector to another may be a market choice as far as initial (high-income) movers are concerned; but it becomes progressively a coerced exchange as the residual mode or sector shrinks to an uneconomic size, or changes character as choice if reduced, or becomes a low-status, under-financed refuge of the disadvantaged alone, or simply becomes progressively more costly and less efficient. (Dunleavy, 1983, p. 25)

The processes involved in this type of exchange relationship and sectoral and/or modal exiting are complex, but Dunleavy is arguing that the mechanisms by which social consumption plays a strategic role in market societies is through compulsory consumption and coerced exchange. The social structure of these societies is, therefore, constantly shifting in the wake of social consumption processes, while the economies become increasingly dependent on the complementary production of new demands and the extension of unmet wants, generally implying a sustained level of commitment to socialised consum-ption outlays. Conventional analysis of cuts and the withdrawal of public spending from service provision in recent years should rather be read as shifts in exchange relationships. For example, the widespread sale of council houses since 1980 should be seen not as a process of 'recommodification' (returning or diverting public assets into the private sector), but as a switch of resources from one sub-type of socialised consumption to another; that is to say, according to Dunleavy's classification of consumption processes, from a purely 'collective consumption' category (where access is judged by criteria of need) to 'quasi-individual-ised consumption' (where services are privately supplied but marketed with a subsidy).

Dunleavy's early and more recent analyses of socialised consumption both offer important contributions to understand-ing current social system divides which are generated by state-provided services and state subsidisation programmes. The early analysis points to the significance of public/private divides (particularly for voting alignments, although the claim that this approach supersedes conventional voting behaviour analysis has yet to be confirmed), while the recent position shows the long-run process of state intervention in socialised consumption by subsidising both the public and private sectors.

Other writers have been less successful in developing Castells's collective consumption thesis. Saunders, for example, in an analysis of the meaning and social significance of the growth of owner occupation argues that the move towards privatised solutions to service provision involves the withdrawal of state subsidies and a relatively easy transition for most people to greater reliance on private modes of provision (Sunders, 1984; see also Harloe, 1984, for a critical appraisal of Saunders). Saunders misses a crucial feature of Dunleavy's argument, namely that state subsidisation is flexibly attached to provision in both sectors and, indeed in owner occupation is witnessing an expanding level of expenditure on tax concessions for mortgagees. But Dunleavy may be wrong to assert that 'Modal and sectoral shifts involve substitutions of one product by another *which delivers basically the same benefits*, or basic changes in the organisation and financing of the same product' (emphasis added). It may be the case that 'exiting' from one sector to another, even if it is a relatively coerced exchange, confers qualitative advantages and not merely sustaining standards, as Dunleavy implies. For example, access to owner occupation through the 'right to buy' legislation provides access to an accruing capital asset. This characteristic of home ownership, although historically not always the case, seems likely to continue for some time. It implies a growing profile of an autonomous cache of private wealth filtering into the economy through 'leakage' (equity withdrawal) or at the point of inheritance. The Building Societies Association estimated that in 1979 alone, £4.5 billion was realised by people selling for the last time. What happens to this money? Much will certainly go back into housing – to sponsor moves up the housing ladder (Murie and Forrest, 1980) – but some will go into commodity purchase and the purchase of private health care, private education, private pensions, and so on. The implication of this is that for the increasing number of people with access to housing wealth, dependence on socialised consumption provision may be short-circuited. In the longer run, when owner occupation has reached saturation point, housing will remain a major source of access to autonomous resources for beneficiaries, people who choose to 'trade down' the market, or who move from the south to the north (from expensive to cheaper areas).

In the context of sectoral consumption politics, the type of wealth-creating process overlays, and to some extent, counteracts Dunleavy's notion of an upward trend in socialised consumption spending. But the equations and long-term implications of housing wealth and the consumption process are beyond the scope of this analysis. The central concern here is to point to the existence of a range of public/private sectoral divisions as social bases and the existence of urban movements rooted in them. Dunleavy's work has clarified Castells's original notion of collective consumption to the point where it is now analytically functional. In terms of urban social movements there is a close link between sectoral consumption issues which unite or divide people according to their mode of access to key services, creating distinct material advantages and disadvantages. There has been a large number of prominent issues in recent years that are basically sectoral clashes that cut across the social class spectrum. For example, within the health services there have been campaigns to develop and expand private medicine and, on the other hand, the action against 'pay beds' run by the NHS trade unions has been prominent; in the transport and road services private hauliers have exerted strong pressures to increase loads, while conservationists point to the destructive potential of heavy trucks on local environments; in housing, the council house tenants' movement argues for increased spending on the maintenance and repair of the public housing stock; ratepayer groups campaign for more efficient local government services, call for rate reductions and the extension of private sector involvement in public service provision. Many of these issues have a locality dimension, but essentially the focus is on movements and campaigns concerned with the provision of services within the public and private sectors, creating conflicts of interest.

Having argued for the existence of major cross-cutting consumption divisions, it remains to examine the mobilisation processes that generate or inhibit social movement formation within these social bases.

Consumption politics and social process

In the same way that residential communities as social bases are bound up with pre-existing associational networks, so it can be shown that consumption interests are mediated by a range of control mechanisms. The evidence for this is sparse, but is well illustrated in work by Rex arising out of the 'housing class' thesis (Rex and Moore, 1967). Although their analysis has a strong spatial dimension, suggesting affinity to the community studies, the thrust of Rex and Moore's work concerns the social and economic processes of the inner-city housing market, leading to the creation of distinct consumption interests. The urban social system, they suggest, is predicated by the forces that shape the housing market,

> that the basic process underlying urban social interaction is competition for scarce and desired types of housing. In this process people are distinguished from one another by their strength in the housing market, or more generally in the system of housing allocation. (Rex and Moore, 1967, p. 274)

In the specific context of inner-city Birmingham in the mid-1960s, Rex and Moore distinguished seven main housing class situations: the outright owners of large houses in desirable areas, mortgagees who occupy whole houses in desirable areas, council house tenants, council tenants in slum dwellings awaiting demolition, tenants of whole houses owned by a private landlord, owners of houses bought with short-term loans compelled to let rooms to meet their repayments, and the tenants of rooms in lodging-houses.

While the notion of housing classes has been subject to some justifiable criticism (Haddon, 1970; Saunders, 1979) a crucial element in this work has largely been overlooked: if there are objectively defined housing classes – which we take as a form of consumption cleavage – what is the likelihood of the members of a particular class subjectively recognising their shared interest and, beyond this, of a housing class mobilising to defend or advance its interest?

In answer to this, Rex and Moore suggest that there is an

integrative mechanism that blurs to varying degrees the conflict inherent in competition for scarce housing facilities and also conflict in the wider social and industrial system. First, they discovered in Sparkbrook a system 'of status grading of the ways of life of various neighbourhoods' in which people would aspire from a lower to a higher position, and presumably would have different insights into and knowledge of the facts of the hierarchy. This is not unlike the status systems observed in our analysis of the community studies in the previous section. Second, because Sparkbrook is an area with a large immigrant population, the formation of housing classes 'might be overlaid and distorted by another fundamental process in which immigrants into the city form colonies which provides the means to partial temporary pluralistic integration'. From the security of this base they can launch out into the wider social and cultural system of urban life. But it is the particular stage of colony formation that provides an alternative form of consciousness to housing class interests.

In reconciling the potential conflicts in the housing class system and in providing for the expression of ethnic, religious or political values, Rex and Moore saw as particularly significant the multiplicity of voluntary associations that exist in the area. Whether political parties, churches, tenants', immigrants' or community associations, they all provide, at least in part, the means by which special interests can be advanced and through which aggressive or defensive sentiments can be harnessed and 'institutionalised'. Among the different ethnic communities they found a considerable variation in the ability to utilise and adapt their organisational life: the Irish have an established colony structure providing a good basis for assimilation; the West Indians were handicapped by having fewer organisational ties and by racial discrimination; the Pakistanis were culturally and racially distinct but well organised to defend and promote their separate interests. 'It is out of the interaction of these three groups with an English community in a decaying urban district that Sparkbrook's social system has to be fashioned' (Rex and Moore, 1967, p. 172).

In a later article Rex develops this theme by suggesting that a key feature of voluntary associations in the inner-city context is the way in which, through them, the values and meaning systems of the immigrant colonies are externalised. The point of specific interest is that the organisation of housing classes into a conscious force may be sought in the study of urban voluntary associations: 'The area in which one would begin to look for a partial development of housing classes so that they become classes-for-themselves is in the study of organisations, norms, beliefs, values and sentiments of the associations, which exist in profusion in the city' (Rex, 1973, p. 39). All the organisations in Sparkbrook – churches, drinking clubs, community associations, etc. – play a number of roles irrespective of their explicit function in overcoming isolation, acting as 'trade unions' on behalf of their members, providing pastoral care and 'elaborating new meanings, norms and belief systems'. The second of these functions particularly suggests the emergence of a 'class-for-itself', while the social functions of the organisations are more closely related to the development of the colony structure. The associations should be understood, therefore, 'as the agencies either of incipient housing-classes-for-themselves or of immigrant colonies' (Rex, 1973, p. 39).

Two key points for the analysis of urban conflict and social change may be extracted from Rex's material. First, that having identified housing classes as an objective feature of the urban social system, members of particular housing classes are subject to a variety of alternative sources of consciousness that overlie the housing market itself. In an inner-city 'immigrant' area, the colony structure expressed through a variety of associational forms absorbs most of the inherent social and economic conflict; there may be no collective consciousness of belonging to a particular housing class. Second, not only is there an absence of collective consciousness, but there appears to be no readily available organisational structure within which a housing class can become, in the Marxist formulation, a 'class-for-itself'. Any functions that may surface are readily absorbed by the group world.

In this section two major sources of potential social base formation, residential communities and consumption cleavages, have been examined. Both of these are targeted by public and private sector agencies and harbour potential to generate urban social movements. But implicit within the notion of mobilisation is the importance of cross-cutting associational activity that stifles collective action or mediates the form the action takes. This field, of the sociology of social bases, is largely ignored by Castells, but is crucial to our understanding of the mobilisation process.

Ideologies of the urban system

Within the urban political system there is a range of ideologies that condition the terms on which urban social movements develop. They establish very specific parameters for some organisations, particularly on the right of the political spectrum, but all of them are subject to the effects of a process of ideological structuring.

A key ideology in the British context is the strong, constitutionally enshrined attachment to a system of democratic control over local government. It is a central orthodoxy of our political system (Dearlove, 1979). It asserts that local government is not just democratic, but that it is somehow an especially democratic part of our wider polity. This notion is a throwback to the attachment to the local control of local government by the dominant elites in the nineteenth century. The notion of locality has endured, and there is also a sense in which much of the politics of local government can be read as an attempt to re-capture elite control over the local level. Certainly much of the practice of local government is focused on elite groups despite the claims of the orthodoxy. A typical statement of this orthodoxy was made by the Royal Commission investigating local government in London in the mid-1960s. They asserted that 'control of the expert by the amateur representing his fellow citizens is the key to our system of (local) government'. But factual analysis does not support such a view, in particular because virtually all the evidence we have describes a political system that is effectively insulated from influence by the 'citizens'. The majority of local councils are one-party states in which the notion of electoral responsiveness through the competition of parties is non-existent. Largely because of this, the internal exercise of power tends to be oligarchic, with a typical power axis shared between a few senior councillors and key officers. For example, in a study of a major functional committee of the Newcastle-Upon-Tyne council, it was found that of the 470 resolutions adopted over a twelve-month period, 89 per cent were recommended by the senior officers supported by the Committee Chairman and only 11 per cent resulted from the intervention of backbench councillors (and most of those were uncontroversial amendments). Ordinary backbenchers had little influence because of the control of information by the officers and the timing of its release, the short duration of pre-committee meetings and the effect of party discipline (Green, 1981). In a party-dominated local government system, the focal arena of policy ratification, and to some extent formulation, is not the full council meeting but rather the group meeting of the majority party councillors. Council meetings are the visible rather than the effective forum of local government, rubber-stamping ruling party policy and where the theatre of local politics is enacted primarily for the benefit of the media.

The portrayal of councillors as the focal point of the system of 'representative' democracy is a misconception not only because their influence on policy is marginal, but also because there is no agreement about what representation actually entails. The view of the Conservative Party Central Office, for example, is that they 'are opposed to the system of delegates . . . all members and representatives of the Conservative Party are free to speak and vote according to their conscience'. An alternative perspective is suggested by Bevan, who wrote that 'the elected person (should) speak with the authentic voice of those who elected him' (Bevan, 1952). Neither position, however, adequately describes the reality of local politics. Internal party systems of either political complexion are oligarchic and subject to forms of discipline, while Bevan's plea that the social profiles of the representatives should mirror the social composition of the voters as a whole bears little relation to the facts. Manual workers, women and young people are grossly underrepresented on local councils, with only marginal improvement since the 1974 reorganisation of local government.

The orthodox position on the question of representation tends to stress the ability of the person elected. A concern with 'councillor calibre', common in the reforming reports, is said by Dearlove to be a concealed attempt to re-establish a more direct relationship between the dominant economic institutions and the political control of local government, typical of nineteenth

century local administration. Accordingly, emphasis in select-
ing councillors has been placed on their managerial skills and
the internal management systems have been modelled on
business enterprises. Dearlove suggests this is a response to the
rise of the Labour Party in municipal politics from the 1920s
onwards, which was seen as creating a 'problem' for the national
elites (Dearlove, 1979).

Nevertheless the ideological weight of representative democracy is very powerful. It is used to delegitimise urban protest
movements if they are unsympathetic to the controlling party
programme or to specific parts of it. The democratically elected
representatives of whatever political complextion do not easily
or willingly relinquish their position as the formal centre of
political authority in local government. Confronted by this,
outsider groups have either to establish alternative democratic
credentials, by displays of representativeness through public
meetings, petitions or building up a broadly-based 'membership', or they seek the support of 'insiders', which may involve
compromising on their demands. The orthodoxy of local
representative democracy impinges directly on the tactics and
style of urban social movements and can be mobilised to screen
out large areas of public disquiet (Dearlove, 1973; Dunleavy,
1977).

Linked into the orthodoxies of electoral accountability is an
equally pervasive ideology described by Dunleavy as the
'ratepayer ideology'. This concerns both the spending capacity
of local authorities and a tenure-based misconception about the
sources of rate payments. Although rates are not the major
source of funding for local authorities, because they are
extracted on a variable and localised basis to finance locally
provided services, they have a very powerful position within the
local political system. The effect is to exert a managerialist
approach to public services. As Dunleavy suggests, 'The central
thrust of managerialism is fiscal and resource conservatism and
an emphasis on accounting accuracy and budgetary control,
powerfully strengthened by the distinctive audit procedures of
local government' (Dunleavy, 1981, p. 148). Every spending
decision is overlaid either explicitly or implicitly by the
question, 'what will the ratepayers think?' It is here that the
democratic orthodoxy overlaps with the rates issue to produce a

powerful ideological formula. A second strand within the ratepayer ideology concerns the differential perception of the relationship between ratepaying, subsidisation and tenure. At its poles it suggests that council tenants are highly subsidised and pay no rates, while owner occupiers are unsubsidised and pay rates; in fact both are highly subsidised (owners more than tenants) and both pay rates on an identical basis.

The partial structuring of this ideology around the tenures is a potent and pervasive factor in the contemporary phase of social policy development. Current economic policy favours an approach based on the idea of a 'recommodification of capital'; that is to say, in the policy context, to seek private market solutions to providing public services. This has a specific force in the context of the 'right to buy' council houses following the 1980 Housing Act.

But this ideological perspective goes beyond the housing system into the whole spectrum of public service provision. An additional ideological focus is on the public/private provision of local services. Clearly this draws from the same sources as the ratepayer ideology, but is concerned not only with spending policy but with the fundamental question of whether the local authorities should concede services to private market modes of provision. Urban social movements have developed on both sides of this divide, and in particular a substantial network of ratepayer associations, whose political programmes focus on the need to curb 'overspending', to reduce or abolish rates, and to promote the substitution of private market solutions to many areas of service provision.

The emergence of powerful consumption cleavage based on housing seems to be an influential factor on partisan align-ment, but also forms an important structural influence on the extension of private sector choices in service provision. This may result partly from the store of wealth contained in owner occupied housing. As noted earlier in the chapter, the scale of 'leakage' from the assets of owner occupation is massive and mainly occurs when people move house or at the point of inheritance. Private sector services are becoming more accessi-ble in proportion to the expansion of home ownership, due to the cache of resources stored in privately owned housing. This factor and the influences surrounding the ratepayer and public/

private sector ideologies are important factors in the relatively low level of response made to the cuts in public service provision in the late 1970s and 1980s. The sale of council houses, with massive discounts and easy access to mortgage finance, has emerged as the dominant issue within the public housing sector. Consumption cleavages potentially have the greatest impact among manual workers because the divides are more apparent within that social stratum. It is not surprising, therefore, to find strong popular support in many areas for the 'right to buy' policy. The effect has been to create an atmosphere in which public service provision, not only in housing but across the whole range of services, has developed strongly negative connotations. The primacy of housing tenure as a determinant of general attitudes to social welfare (Kemeny, 1980) would seem to account for the low level of mobilisation against the cuts in public services. The collapse of council house building to its lowest level since the 1920s happened in the ideological and political context of a switch in emphasis to private sector provision.

The mobilisation process in the urban system is surrounded by a web of intricate and powerful ideological forces: local democratic accountability through local councils, a ratepayer-based ideology centring on housing tenure divides and a public/private sector ideology. They shape the conditions under which urban social movements evolve and account for the pervasive existence of non-action, organisational retreat and co-option within the urban political process.

Conclusion

In the British context the mobilisation process is structured by a range of core influences that operate to generate and sustain, or to screen out, urban protest. Of particular significance in the latter case is the presence of a labyrinth of existing associational activity that must be harnessed or penetrated if new organisations are to make a sustained impact. There is a dual problem of subjective recognition and an ability and willingness to act collectively. Social base identification is crucial in analytical terms, and two major dimensions have been suggested: residential community and sectoral consumption cleavages. The characteristics of local political systems and the existence of a range of ideologies within these systems crucially affect the genesis of urban social movements, their tactics and organisational forms, and create the specific conditions for the growth of some movements or the absence of, or co-option of, conflict around key issues. These analytical themes were all raised in Castells's work but none of them were systematically explored. They are used in the next two chapters, which analyse types of urban social movements active in Britain in the 1970s and 1980s.

Chapter 4

Public Sector Housing Movements

Council house tenants' associations are common in Britain but are a relatively undocumented form of urban movement. They represent people who are both geographically identifiable as a 'community' (most council housing is built as estates), and also the public wing of the sectoral divide in housing. This chapter describes the social base characteristics of council housing, reviews the available evidence on the nature and characteristics of tenants' associations, and describes the origins and subsequent evolution of a large-scale tenants' movement in Sheffield. The Sheffield tenants' movement has been in existence since the late 1960s and has evolved through a number of phases. This life-cycle demonstrates the necessity for detailed and sustained longitudinal analysis if the relationship between the social base and the organisational form, and between patterns of evolution and dissolution, are to be understood.

Council estates as social bases

Tenants of public housing are a particularly unified and identifiable social base, although the introduction of the 'right to buy' in the 1980 Housing Act is beginning to break the solidaristic form of the base in some areas (Murie and Forrest, 1984). There are three main components involved in the structuring of the council tenants social base. First, these tenants are the subjects of highly restrictive managerial processes and share a range of common material interests. Council housing is a non-market housing system theoretically based on 'need' but in reality determined by complex managerial vetting of the applicants prior to allocation (Gray, 1979). Subsequently the householders become tenants of a public landlord whose tenancy arrangements are tightly drawn. There is in addition a high degree of spatial concentration of council tenants into distinctive built environments. Council 'estates' are immediately identifiable in any part of the country. Over 70 per cent of high-rise flat accommodation is council owned.

A second set of characteristics of public housing as a social base concerns the very strong ideological structuring that surrounds the tenure. This is particularly encapsulated in the ratepayer ideology – the misconceived view of council housing as a highly subsidised tenure that is funded disproportionately from the locally paid rates of home owners. More recently an additional and pervasive ideological strand has become prominent. Here a contrast is drawn between, on the one hand, council housing as a form of welfare provision for the very poorest households and, on the other, the notion of council housing as a general and substantial tenure, providing a genuine alternative to home ownership for a broad band of socio-economic strata. In fact, council housing does now contain a very high proportion of families on supplementary benefits and in the lowest quartile of income distribution, overwhelmingly in the manual worker occupations. This tendency has accelerated since the war, and since the late 1970s has been underpinned by government encouragement for the sale of the council stock. The promotion of owner occupancy as the 'natural' and 'desired' form of tenure leads directly to regarding council housing as a residual tenure. The generally low level of opposition to this policy indicates the strength of the ideological formation. Council housing is thus cross-cut by two interlinked ideological systems, one concerning the form of its subsidisation, and the other its status in the overall housing system. Both tend to enforce an essentially negative and defensive self-perception that feeds strongly into the character of the tenants' movement.

Third, public housing in Britain is characterised by an overwhelmingly working-class social and cultural milieu. Some of the forms and consequences this has for associational activity were discussed in the section on community studies in Chapter 2.

Taken together these strands sustain a strongly defined social base which under certain circumstances mobilises into a social movement. There is a rich but virtually undocumented tradition of militant tenants' movements acting in defence of shared interests, particularly over the rents issue. But collective action also involves less radical bargaining procedures with public sector agencies and with housing departments over living costs and conditions. Finally, the analytical focus on this social base also extends to the study of the evidence of non-action on important and pervasive policy issues.

Tenants' associations in Britain

Tenants' associations are relatively difficult to analyse because they straddle these mobilisation characteristics and must also be read in the context of the interaction between the social base elements – bureaucratic allocation and management procedures, the blend of ideologies, and the social system characteristics on the estates. They tend to have relatively unstructured organisational forms and to operate on the periphery of the formal political system. Often the distinction between associations oriented to programmes of social events and those that are more directly 'political' is difficult to make. There are no studies of these organisations across a time span of more than a few months. This leads to the impression that tenants' organisations are a superficial and eclectic form of urban protest. But this is mainly a problem of faulty research methodologies and funding, and applies across the whole range of urban social movements. This gap in the urban studies literature is a serious omission. As Dunleavy observes,

> The analysis of urban social movements may hold the key to the intractable problems of studying non-protest and quiescence in urban politics . . . It may also afford insights into the mechanisms of ideological stabilisation which limit the development of broader political movements from organisations around urban issues. (Dunleavy, 1980, pp. 158–9)

A common assumption arising from the lack of evidence and the generally low visibility of urban social movements in local politics is that they are issue-specific and tend to disintegrate as quickly as they appear (Goldsmith, 1982). This may often be the case, although the evidence is speculative; but in cases where there is a deep-rooted social base, the life-cycles of the movements are more complex and sustained. The dissolution of organisations is not inevitable or predetermined and may have specific causes not necessarily related to the issue. Similarly, attempts to account for the life-cycle of urban social movements by reference either to a continuous upswing in urban protest in the 1980s (Castells, 1983) or to the suggestion of a 'lull' in activity in the late 1970s (Ceccarelli, 1982; Pickvance, 1983) should be read against social base characteristics as well as the 'conjunctural' stage at the political level. Otherwise it is possible that our understanding of the mechanisms of urban social change, and the stabilisation and containment of protest, may be side-tracked.

In the case of the council house tenants' movement in Sheffield there was a clear formative issue, but the development of the movement and its component organisations over a period of more than fifteen years (from 1967 to date) involved definite patterns of evolution related to the characteristics of the estates and the repercussions within the local state system of the early tenants' movement. What were the issues that generated the growth of this movement? Under what circumstances did the social base mobilise? And having entered the local political system, what then happened to it and what effects did it have? The case study is prefaced with a short review of the little evidence there is of the nature and characteristics of the tenants' movement in Britain.

The tenants' movement

Tenants' associations and federations of tenants' organisations exist and have existed in Britain in their thousands. But very little has been written about them and much of the evidence is in the oral tradition of working-class history, which does not easily lend itself to academic analysis but is a deeply ingrained source of political experience. As will be shown, the tenants' movement is inherent within the consumption 'location' of council house tenants, but in its most politically potent form consists of organisations which do not exist continuously. They operate on the periphery of the formal party political system in local government, are instrumental to a relatively small range of issues, and tend to make only sporadic appearances. There are no studies of this type of tenants' organisation over extended time periods, although there is some documentation of a number of specific campaigns (Hampton, 1970; Moorhouse *et al.*, 1972; Sklair, 1975). A second type of tenants' association, often developing out of an issue-based organisation, has recieved rather more detailed attention in the community studies and community work literature (Lupton and Mitchell, 1954; Goetschius, 1969; Henderson *et al.*, 1982). These 'established' associations are mainly based on social and leisure activities, often involving management responsibility for a tenants' hall. It will be argued that these groups also represent the incipient consumption interests of tenants, but more partially, and potentially act to screen out urban protest. At the very least it may be more difficult to re-create militant protest from within existing and semi-institutionalised organisations.

The most celebrated and most written about tenants' movement is that of tenants of private landlords in Glasgow in 1915, cited by Castells and mentioned in Chapter 1 (Middlemas, 1964; Melling, 1979 and 1980; Castells, 1983). It involved thousands of tenants in a ferociously fought rent strike against landlords, who took the opportunity of war conditions – men away fighting in the trenches and a scarcity of accommodation caused by an influx of munitions workers – to increase rents. The involvement in this action of large numbers of women and of the emergent shop stewards' movements in the factories were the crucial features of this movement. The political sensitivity of the area, because of the munitions industry, led to government intervention to freeze rents at pre-war levels. The impact of the rent strike on national housing policy has been the subject of some controversy. But it is undeniable that in the special circumstances of the war, government for the first time implemented a national scheme of rent controls from which successive governments have been unable to extricate themselves. It was hardly expedient for a government to greet their returning armies with a bout of rent increases (Bowley, 1945). For the same reason the 1919 election campaign slogan of 'Homes Fit For Heroes' also led to increased government intervention into the housing market. As Malpass and Murie observe,

Private builders who had virtually abandoned working-class housing as an unprofitable undertaking before the war could not return to it unless it could be made to pay, which meant higher rates or state subsidies. (Malpass and Murie, 1982, p. 32)

The period from the mid-1920s until the outbreak of the Second World War saw a massive programme of nationally subsidised but local authority-built and owned housing. Every main centre of population had its 'council estates' and with them began the era of the council house tenants' movement.

As a sociological analysis of a council estate Durant's (1939) study of the Watling Estate has not yet been superseded. A number of lower level studies followed in the 1940s and 1950s (Morris and Mogey, 1954; Lupton and Mitchell, 1954), all of which contained reference to the early establishment of tenants' associations on the newly built estates. These associations had the functions of assisting in the 'settling down' process and undertaking negotiations with the local housing authorities on environmental and management problems. The hostile reaction of the host communities is frequently quoted as another reason for the development of solidaristic tenants' associations (Collison, 1963). Frankenberg's reading of the literature leads him to believe that there is a common pattern to these events:

There is a familiar pattern of initial loneliness followed by unity against the outside world giving rise to an agitational Residents' Association. This achieves its tasks and most of the inhabitants settle down to a home-centred but small group orientated social life . . . A minority continues the public life of the community centre. This minority is drawn from one status group. (Frankenberg, 1966, p. 214)

The tendency for protest associations to turn into social organisations is a common thread running through the history of the tenants' movement, but as we have suggested, this is by no means the whole story with these metamorphosed groups. It should also be made clear that many of the most militant tenants' associations are transient and leave few traces, either organisational or documentary.

The inter-war period saw the growth of thousands of residents' and tenants' associations on the new private and public housing estates. These were linked mainly to initial problems of services, management and a wider socialisation process. But most militant tenants' activity was still confined to the private rental sector, which housed the poorest families in the worst conditions. There was, for example, a large-scale and prolonged rent strike of private tenants in the East End of London in the late 1930s. After the war private renting dwindled rapidly as a tenure and the political force it contained was as a result fragmented.

The council house tenants' movement, however, began to establish itself. A communist-backed national organisation, the National Association of Tenants and Residents (NATR) was set up in 1948 and continued to be active into the mid-1970s. The Association of London Housing Estates, established in 1957, represented a large number of socially orientated associations and has a continuous record of activity up to the present time, currently under the title of the London Tenant's Organisation. But regional or national federations are difficult to sustain, requiring either subsidisation from public funds, strongly implying a non-political orientation to their activity, or they find it hard to establish and retain credibility with individual associations. It is at city or borough level, rather than at regional or national level, where federations have had their greatest impact.

There is little evidence of militant tenants' action in the 1950s, but by the early 1960s a number of local authorities were planning to revise their rent structures in order to help balance the chronic state of their housing revenue account. The drift towards establishing 'market' levels of rents for council house tenants was also gathering pace, but the debts incurred by many authorities as a result of their building programmes was the primary reason for the generally increased and increasing levels of rent payments. An early example of a tenants' movement based on a restructuring and increased level of rents, which included a means-tested rebate scheme, occurred in the London borough of St. Pancras in 1960 (Moorhouse *et al.*, 1972). Delegates from thirty-five individual associations joined together in the United Tenants' Association under the slogan 'not a penny on the rents' – the famous slogan from the 1915 Glasgow incident which was to become popularised in the big GLC tenants' rent strike in the late 1960s. Following implementation, some 1400 tenants were officially acknowledged as withholding rent payments. A number of attempted evictions of strike leaders led to violent scenes outside St. Pancras Town Hall – fifty people were arrested – and the Home Secretary banned marches in the area for three months. After a succession of attempts at a negotiated solution the heavy-handed threat of evictions broke the rent strike and the movement collapsed.

On a national scale the tenants' movement reached a post-war zenith during a five-year period from 1968 to 1973. This phase of intensive activity centred on two main issues, both originating from central government policy: the imposition of means-tested rebates in the context of restructured rent levels, and second, the campaign against the Housing Finance Act which extended and consolidated the trend towards market levels of rents (so-called 'fair rents').

In 1967 the Labour government reached a nadir in its political fortunes. The economic crisis forced a devaluation of the pound. At the local government level 1967 and 1968 were almost the worst years ever for Labour since they became a major force in municipal politics in the mid-1920s. In April 1967 the Conservatives took control of the GLC by a landslide majority; and it was in response to their attempts to control the imbalances in the housing revenue account and to reduce subsidies from the rates to council tenants that a massive explosion of tenants' activity took place in the capital city. The proposal of the new council was to introduce a system of 'fair rents' in line with the method for assessing the rents of private tenants under the 1965 Housing Act. In London this meant that rents would rise by nearly 70 per cent over a three-year period. The worst off tenants were to be partly screened from the effects of these rises by the introduction of means-tested rebates. Action began almost immediately, and 'not a penny on the rents' leaflets were widely circulated. Ten estates in Tower Hamlets formed a federation of tenants' asociations. A federation in Hackney called for joint action against the GLC, and a United Tenants' Action Committee was set up (Moorhouse *et al.*, 1972, pp. 140–1). During the summer of 1968 a variety of marches and mass lobbies took place. In Tower Hamlets 2000 people lobbied a council meeting to persuade the Labour-controlled authority not to evict tenants for non-payment of rent increases and to provide accommodation for people evicted from other boroughs. By November 1968, a month after implementation of the scheme, the GLC's own figures suggested that as many as 11,000 households were on partial rent strike by withholding the increases. In the new year many of the tenants were warned in a letter from the Housing Director that they faced imminent eviction if they withheld due rent. This provocation lead to a series of incidents including a demonstration of 3000 people outside the Housing Minister's home in Hampstead. Further threats of evictions during the summer months of 1969 led to the establishment of an Anti-Eviction Committee, which promised industrial action, especially in the London docks, and organised a vigilante group said to contain 700 men to act as a 'flying squad' in the event of eviction threats (Moorhouse *et al.*, 1972, p. 142). In November 1969 the government passed legislation limiting rises to an average of 7s 6d a week. It seems likely that this step was taken in the face of the extensive action by the GLC tenants, especially in the East End. The rent strike itself ended in confusion and acrimony in the spring of 1970 after unsuccessful legal action against the GLC which sought to test the validity of their eviction procedures. This change of direction, to legal action, seems to have been a desperate last attempt by the leaders of the tenants' movement to sustain the rent strike, but it had the effect of diverting attention away from any form of direct action.

Although on a small scale, but still extensive in relation to the populations of council tenants, many city and borough councils faced similar protest action by their tenants. The local authorities varied in their methods, but most regarded it as essential to cover the deficits on the Housing Revenue Account, usually by differential rent schemes and the imposition of rent increases with cushioning rebates for poor families. There is evidence of action by tenants from as far apart as Exeter to Glasgow. The Sheffield tenants' movement discussed in the case study in this chapter originated in this context. In Liverpool the increases provoked a rent strike which lasted six months and actually won a small reduction in the increase; but in general mass tenants' action was not successful in preventing the drift towards market levels of rent and means-tested rebates.

A final wave of militant protest on this basic issue flared up on a national basis against the Conservative government's Housing Finance Act; the 'fair rent' Act. This legislation had the effect of consolidating the existing situation of generally rising rent levels to bring council house tenants formally in line with the fair rent assessment that had existed for private tenants since 1965. The notion of public housing as non-market accommodation based on criteria of need was finally eclipsed by the 1972 Housing Finance Act. It did not pass into statute, however, without a second round of extensive action, not only by tenants but also by a large number of dissenting Labour-controlled local authorities who rather belatedly stood their ground. Some forty-five local authorities refused initially to implement the Act. And although the efforts of the NATR to organise a national campaign was not widely supported – only 3000 attended their London rally in October 1972 – there is documentary evidence from over eighty individual local authorities of rent strikes by council tenants (Sklair, 1975). The situation nationally was complex because of the refusal of many Labour-controlled authorities to implement the legislation. Against this the legislation threatened authorities with possible takeover by Housing Commissioners, and individual councillors with the prospect of having to fund deficits caused by uncollected rent from their own pockets. As Sklair points out, the stage was set for a massive anti-government campaign. The Conservatives had lost nearly 3000 seats in the local elections of 1971 and 1972, but the Labour Party was too slow in co-ordinating its campaign, and possibly lacked the political will for a major confrontation. By the time initiatives had been taken – notably by Sheffield City Council – many authorities had already decided to implement the legislation. In the end, only three authorities never implemented the Act, Clay Cross, Bedwas and Machen. After the failure of the Labour and trade union movement to stop the Bill and to organise effectively a non-implementation campaign, it was left to thousands of tenants, organised in their own associations, to protest through rent strikes. Sklair identified a clear correlation between the existence of rent strike activity and whether or not the local authority had fought against the implementation:

> 80 per cent of the rent strikes occurred in places where the Labour Council implemented the Act in good time . . . it looks almost as if tenants' militancy, as measured by the will to withhold rent, is rather more likely to manifest itself where the council quietly implements than where it puts up a fight. (Sklair, 1975, p. 268)

Where councils resisted, the tenants' movement mainly restricted its activity, to supporting action via the council chamber. This is an important finding, partly because it indicates that tenants will take the line of least resistance, given the option of falling in line with a Labour Party campaign, and partly because it indicates the narrow range of options available for independent tenants' action.

There is little doubt that the vast majority of Labour councillors, when faced with the prospect of defying the law and threatened with personal surcharges, had no hesitation in implementing the Act. In some areas, especially small towns in the solid Labour-supporting areas of the North of England and Wales and frequently controlled by right-wing Labour councillors, the tenants' movement was intimidated into quick submission by threats of eviction. In other areas the tactics were different. One of the largest and most sustained partial rent strikes occurred in the West Midlands town of Dudley. At the height of their action the Dudley Tenants' Association (a federation of some thirty groups) had 15,000 tenants withholding an 80p increase. As time went by the local Labour Party gradually recruited leading tenants' activists into the party, nervous of the effect of the tenants' movement on their electoral prospects as the local elections approached. This also accounts for their reluctance to take direct action against the rent strikes. But with its head partly severed the strike collapsed. Probably the largest action took place in Kirby, where tenants on the Tower Hill estate organised a much more militant campaign with flying pickets, block committees, and a *total* rent strike. The International Socialists played a key role in this action, although not a dominating one. In these circumstances the local council adopted a strategy of harassment.

After the collapse of protest against the Housing Finance Act the tenants' movement went into a decline. A degree of activity re-emerged in the late 1970s in response to some new issues – the possibility of a tenants' charter, dampness, repairs and heating being the main concerns. The rents issue had been decisively lost and was largely stripped from the tenants' movement agenda. A number of skeletal federations persisted, and a conference held in 1977 and sponsored by the National Consumer Council reinvigorated ideas about regional federations and groupings of tenants as a means of developing campaigns. The North East Tenants' Organisation was established as a direct consequence of the conference. The federation in Sheffield was revitalised. A South Wales Association of Tenants was formed. At a national level the National Tenants' Organisation and a less formal body, the National Housing Liaison Committee, both sought to build links across the country. The tactics and style of this renewed movement is, however, very different from the large-scale rent strikes of the earlier period. Street theatre, lobbying behind the scenes, some low key demonstrations and publicity events are the methods of the new tenants' movement. Two exceptions to this generally more conciliatory and passive approach occurred in Walsall and Kirklees in the early 1980s, when rent strike action again took place against large rent increases. But a nationally organised march and rally in Walsall in March 1982 could muster an attendance of only 2000, and although impressive as an event, hardly compared with the vast demonstrations that could be assembled even in single cities in the late 1960s.

The introduction of the 'right to buy' in the 1980 Housing Act and the large-scale buying of council houses that followed was resisted by some local authorities, and the pattern here was for tenants' federations to link into 'joint' campaigns with local Labour Parties and trade unions. But the undoubted popularity of the right to buy, posed as the ultimate in tenants' rights by the Conservative government, has fragmented the social base and the ideological unity of council tenants. There may well be a backlash against this policy as some of the problems as well as benefits of home ownership become apparent. At this time the tenants' movement is in a very defensive position and unable to make substantive progress even on the issues of repairs, dampness and heating, due to the collapse of the public sector spending programme. The focus of policy-making has shifted decisivly to central government, against which the tenants' movement is at its weakest and most vulnerable.

This account of the phases in the tenants' movement only partially expresses the themes that underlie and moulded its progress. Each association or federation of associations responded tactically to the decisions made in the local, party-dominated political arenas. The ideological strands were particularly potent in this history of development and retrenchment. The move in the post-1945 era from 'reluctant collectivist' to positively 'anti-collectivist' (George and Wilding, 1976) approaches to council housing strongly influenced the issues on which the tenants' movement was forged, and in the early 1970s blunted its most militant phase. The theme which is least apparently influential in this pattern of events is that relating the social base characteristics of the estates to the establishment and progress of, and the organisational types within, the tenants' movement. It is only possible to describe this in the context of a specific case study rather than a generalised narrative. The case to be considered is the tenants' movement in Sheffield. Sheffield is typical of the medium-sized cities of the north of England. It has a high proportion of manual workers in its population and many of these are skilled workers in engineering and steel-making. The city council has been controlled almost continuously by the Labour party since the mid-1920s and has a long history of municipal provision of the urban public services. Sheffield also has one of the highest proportions of council housing in the country, and it is in the dozens of council estates, large and small, that the tenants' movement is rooted.

The tenants' movement in Sheffield (1967–84)

The upsurge of tenants' association activity in Sheffield in 1967 resulted from the decision by the Labour-controlled city council to adopt a rebated rent scheme in line with the national recommendations. There was widespread hostility to the means-tested rebates, but the inclusion in the scheme of an adult occupier surcharge, popularly known as the 'lodger tax', including teenage children in employment, was thought to be particularly iniquitous. It was this issue that exploded into the political life of the city in the first few months of 1967, saw the establishment of tenants' associations on all the main estates, and was responsible for the Labour Party losing control of the city council for only the second time since Labour took power in 1926 (Lowe, 1977).

Initially reaction was muted and mainly confined to expressions of hostility to the scheme at the Trades Council. The first tenants' association was formed on a pre-war estate in January 1967 by a small group of women. They had no political affiliations and simply knew each other as neighbours. By March they had organised a membership approaching 500. As word of the planned scheme spread across the estates, more associations were formed. The original group, assisted by Trades Council activists, mounted a rally at the City Hall and in the aftermath of this resounding meeting at least ten more associations were inaugurated. Public meetings were crucial to the spread of the movement across the city because they facilitated contacts between the activists and an exchange of experiences about the mood of the tenants and ideas about the practicalities of organising associations. A small group of initiators found that they could produce an organisation sometimes thousands strong in a matter of a few days. There was an infectious quality about the growth of the tenants' movement once news of the early responses spread. Within a few weeks of the first City Hall rally most of the main estates had a tenants' association.

While there is no doubt that this was a spontaneous social movement, the Communist Party made a significant contribution to the spread of the associations by taking a lead in setting up meetings and organising committees. Sheffield has a long history of communist activity, based in the engineering industry, and the city is one of their remaining stronghold areas. At a later stage their involvement, inflamed by an antagonistic press, resulted in a split in the tenants' movement; but at an early stage all strands of opinion, including the majority of 'non-political' tenants' activists (Hampton, 1970), recognised the need for the movement to be co-ordinated on a city-wide basis. Following the City Hall rally, representatives of half a dozen associations met to discuss tactics, and from this meeting the Sheffield Federation of Tenants' Associations was formed. Despite this display of unity there was already disagreement about the means to be employed to defeat the rebate scheme. One faction favoured a cautious and relatively passive approach using conventional pressure group tactics. A more militant line, supported by a clear majority of associations at this stage, argued for mass action, including the use of a rent strike to force the council into submission.

Although under increasing pressure from the Labour and trade union movement in the city, the Labour group of councillors, having deferred implementation of the rebate plan for three months, finally decided to introduce it. The scheme became operational at the beginning of October 1967 and the threatened rent strike began almost immediately. But the divisions among the tenants' organisations were sharpened by their failure to stop the scheme. The rent strike struggled through the winter of 1967–8, but with a growing uncertainty about tactics. The involvement of the communists in the tenants' movement at this point became the focal issue and led to a split in the Federation. Five of the thirteen associations affiliated to the city-wide body broke away to form a new 'Democratic Federation', called off the rent strike in their areas, and prepared to put up independent tenants' candidates at the local elections in May 1968. It was the decision to put up candidates at the elections that precipitated the split in the Federation. The communists planned to run their own candidates, as they had done for decades, and their opposition to the idea of tenants' candidates led to the accusation that they were hiding behind the tenants' movement for their own electoral advantage. For some non-communist tenants' activists the notion of putting up candidates against Labour was not acceptable.

In fact the five tenants' candidates made little impact. The most successful campaign was fought by one of the women from the original association. In a ward containing a high proportion of council houses, and with the tenants' association membership reaching over 3000 at the time, she won only 631 votes, 17.2 per cent of the poll in the ward. The local elections of 1967 and 1968 were held against a background of massive national anti-Labour swings. Not since the early 1930s had Labour been so unpopular at the local level. In Sheffield the addition of a potent local issue produced a cumulative swing against Labour sufficient for them to lose a number of 'safe' seats. Swings against Labour were particularly high in wards with a high proportion of council housing (Lowe, 1980, p. 82). This was caused mainly by Labour abstentions and some votes switching to the Conservatives. Labour won only eight of a possible twenty-seven seats and lost control of the council as a result. The Conservatives had promised in their election manifesto to abolish the 'lodger tax' and revise the new rent structure in favour of the older estates. A small concession was thus won by the tenants' movement, but the substantive issue, of ameliorating the switch to market levels of rent, with rebates for poor families, was lost.

The next phase of the tenants' movement in Sheffield, from 1969 to the mid-1970, was marked by renewed attempts to form a unified movement, the collapse of some of the most militant associations on the older estates, but the consolidation of many others around programmes of social activity, welfare rights advocacy and bargaining with the local authority over estate issues.

The two federations quickly saw the need to re-unite the city-wide movement, partly to accommodate partly to match the changed attitude of Labour to the tenants in the aftermath of their chastening electoral defeat. The Sheffield Federation of Tenants' Associations initially strengthened contacts with the communist-backed National Federation of Tenants' Associations, while the Democratic Federation spent time informally discussing with Labour Party representatives policy issues and forms of liaison between the tenants' movement and the Labour Party. Representatives from both federations went on the huge demonstration of council tenants in London on 22 September 1968, which although ignored by the media was reputed to be one of the biggest marches seen in the capital in the post-war period. Moves to revitalise and unify the movement were subsequently made. In May 1969 a joint Co-ordinating Committee of Tenants' Associations was set up, and despite tensions survived until the mid-1970s.

Labour recaptured control of the city in 1969. It was the only major centre to be returned to Labour control in Labour's worst year since 1931. The promise of a rent freeze for twelve months was widely supposed to have produced a higher than normal turnout and a swing to Labour. Their manifesto included proposals for more tenants' halls and the establishment of a permanent liaison structure between the council and the tenants. This more amicable relationship between the tenants' movement and the Labour group was given added impetus by the new Conservative government's Housing Finance Act (1972). The Co-ordinating Committee organised a campaign against the 'fair rent' Bill (35,000 leaflets were distributed) but it raised little support on the estates. A pattern of rent increases and rebates had already been established and the new legislation appeared to consolidate this trend. Awareness that the local council had to operate under the constraints of central government financial policy was widespread, and the bitter experience of the rent strike was still prevalent. Few individual tenants' associations participated in the Co-ordinating Committee, and by 1974 the group had disintegrated. Until then meetings of the Housing Advisory Committee, the product of the discussion over joint liaison, continued, but it played no constructive role except in legitimising the dialogue between the Labour Party and the tenants' movement. At the meetings the officers would not allow discussion of individual cases and the councillors would not allow discussion of general policy, especially housing finance. The tenants' representatives quickly came to regard the committee as a means of drawing the political sting of the tenants' movement. With the virtual collapse of the Co-ordinating Committee, the Housing Department introduced a system of area consultative committees in a thinly disguised attempt to continue the dialogue, but without the politically threatening influence of a city-wide federation.

The resolution of the rent rebate issue, the collapse of some associations, and the disintegration of the Co-ordinating Committee did not end the tenants' movement in Sheffield. Many individual associations continued to be active, although long-term survival was due to a range of factors only partly connected with the rent issue. This frequently involved the incorporation of the associations into management responsibility for a tenants' hall. Of the surviving associations, 60 per cent mentioned in interview in the mid-1970s the management of a hall as their most important current function (Lowe, 1980, p. 116). A more detailed analysis of the survival of some associations and the collapse of others is made in the next section.

In 1978 a new period of tenants' association activity began in the city. The reasons for this can be traced to a number of national and local sources, and essentially to processes external to the estates. At the national level discussion of a tenants' charter to broaden the rights of council house tenants had been circulating since the late 1960s and had appeared as a small item in Labour's 1977 housing Green Paper. A national conference of tenants' organisations sponsored by the National Consumer Council revitalised the idea for national and regional groupings of tenants' associations. Contacts were made betwen the national organisers and some known activists in Sheffield. But it seems likely that the major impetus to the revival of Sheffield's tenants' movement was created by a number of professional community workers employed by Sheffield local authority's Family and Community Services Committee. These workers had established a number of new associations and reactivated some of the older ones, formerly active in the Co-ordinating Committee. A meeting in February 1978 brought together twenty-seven associations from around the city. A new era in the history of Sheffield's tenants' movement had dawned.

Before the current phase of activity is discussed, it is necessary to move from a narrative account of events to an analysis of the process that shaped the movement in the years following the rent strike. First of all some social science evidence about the evolution of tenants' organisations is examined, and in the light of this the cause of events and the patterns of development in Sheffield are discussed.

Genesis and life-cycles

Despite the wide expansion of council estates from the mid-1920s, the social science literature has a very low level approach to analysis of them and to the organisational form that provide the best evidence of the activity of tenants' associations over reasonably long periods, but the documentation is not sys-tematic and is usually incidental to wider concerns about the anthropology of working-class life (Hodges and Smith, 1954;

Lupton and Mitchell, 1954; see also Frankenberg, 1966, Chapter 8). However, the studies generally observe similar patterns in origins and life-cycles of the associations. These start on new estates in response to the initial problems of isolation and strange surroundings. The hostility of the existing residents, especially middle-class owner occupiers, to the newcomers adds to the sense of solidaristic community. As Durant observes, 'antagonism from without breeds association from within' (Durant, 1939, p. 21). Often the spur to initiating an association is a grievance against the authorities about the management of the estate or lack of facilities. But after a period of militant activity the organisations enter a 'settling down' phase involving a greater emphasis on social activities often associated with the opening of a tenants' hall. The inclusion or not of bar facilities often leads to disputes, and the change of functions is often accompanied by factional and personality disputes within the organisation. This leads to the withdrawal from activity either of the 'respectables' or of lower status groups.

Frankenberg follows Durant in arguing that no matter how militant an association is initially, in the end it settles to a routine round of social activities. But this prescription does not account for deeper level social base characteristics or the fact that consumption issues on housing estates tend to be recurrent. There is a latent solidarism among council tenants which is only mobilised under certain circumstances. A key factor here is that it may be more difficult to mobilise tenants against an issue from a pre-existing associational base. A partial understanding of this basic sociology accounts for the persistent attempts by local authority housing departments to channel the political impetus of the tenants' movement into management responsibility for tenants' hall and community centres. By the same token estates where tenants' associations do not transform into socially based organisations but disintegrate after a political campaign may, in the long term, be better placed to respond to future issues.

As mentioned in Chapter 2, Rex points to the associational world as a mechanism for the absorption of urban-based conflict. But he also points to the functional base of all voluntary associations *vis-à-vis* their members – overcoming loneliness, advocacy and 'trade union' activity, pastoral care, the elaboration of norms and belief systems. It is at this level that the

Durant/Frankenberg perspective on tenants' associations falters. They fail to capture both the specificity of the consumption
location of council house tenants in the urban process and the
sociology of the associational world.

A key point here is that while it may be difficult to rekindle
political action from an established association, the apparent
social orientation adopted by many tenants' organisations
conceals a whole range of advocacy and negotiating functions.
Goetschius, in his fifteen-year study of community groups on
housing estates in London, found that typically tenants' associations played three main roles:

> They provided direct recreation and social welfare services to
> their members . . . secondly, the groups represent the
> membership and the estates in discussion with statutory and
> voluntary bodies . . . thirdly, their work involves the develop-
> ment of social life on the estates (Goetschius, 1969, p. 2)

Similarly, Lupton and Mitchell commented on an association
set up in Liverpool in the early 1940s:

> While its primary purpose was to represent the inhabitants in
> their corporate relations with the outside world, its leaders
> also set themselves the task of giving the estate an internal
> social and recreational unity. (Lupton and Mitchell, 1954)

There are, therefore, a number of themes within the sociology
of community organisation that may be used to inform our
understanding and interpretation of the life-cycles and patterns
of development of council house tenants' associations. Associations may develop from early agitational activity to a settled
routine of social events; this transition may be accompanied by
internal faction fighting among committee members; the established functions may include a 'trade union' role of advocacy and
bargaining on behalf of the membership as well as social events;
there may be a tension surrounding their very existence, held
between their potential to absorb latent and actual conflict in
the urban system and the partial expression of 'housing class'
interest.

The resolution of the rent rebate issue in Sheffield did not lead to the break-up of the tenants' movement but to a second phase of development. In the next section the pattern of this new phase is examined: the collapse of some associations, the continuation of others, and the tactical problems of the tenants' movements as a political force, particularly the difficulties of organising rent strikes and of sustaining city-wide federations of tenants' associations.

Sheffield tenants' associations – establishment and disestablishment

Nearly all the associations that survived into the 1970s did so by changing the orientation of their activity from political action to programmes of social events and of welfare advocacy and bargaining. The general hypothesis outlined by Goetschius was confirmed. This change often involved taking responsibility for running a tenants' hall – the authority built several new ones almost immediately – and organising and managing it became a major task for the activists. There was less internal feuding than might have been expected because the renewed federation gave some of the politicos an outlet for their interests and because it was generally recognised that long-term existence could not be sustained solely on the basis of political activity. A large amount of low-key 'political' action did develop in the form of negotiating with the local authority or other urban public service agencies. The tenants' halls provided good bases for this type of work – office space, a telephone, an address – as well as space for routine leisure activities. In fact, under the umbrella of a bingo session or a club, individuals often found an informal and sympathetic setting for raising issues and individual problems with committee members. It seems that lessons from the past were somehow being learnt, and the pattern identified by Frankenberg of decline into a monotonous round of social events was only a partial reading of tenants' association functions, perhaps appropriate to pre-war experience.

Equally as important as explanations for the metamorphosis of some organisations is an understanding of the failure of others to make this transition. Here the theme of the sociology of the social bases and a detailed understanding of their history and social structures is important. Nearly all the associations that collapsed within the first year of the end of the rent strike were on the older, pre-war estates, and they had also been among the most militant during the rent rebate controversy. Why should this be such a striking pattern? The collapse of the rent strike in some disarray clearly left a legacy of bitterness and demoralisation. Under the terms of the original scheme rent increases were to be the highest on the older estates, and this had the effect of galvanising support for the associations. But underlying the immediate repercussions of what amounted to a defeat, the inability of some of these old estates to sustain their organisation is a result of their social base characteristics. The evidence from the community studies suggests that attitudes to associational activity in established working-class areas are predominantly instrumental. There is little experience of, or interest in, formal organisations, the emphasis instead focusing on the networks of informal interaction. The pre-war estates in Sheffield closely match this general stereotype of stable and established manual worker residential communities. This pattern of social structuring accounts for the speed with which the early associations appeared on the estates – developing rapidly through the mainly female neighbourhood network – but also for their subsequent demise. There is simply no role for them to play in the socialisation process or in the 'pastoral' function identified in Rex's model associations.

Baldock, in an analysis of the Sheffield estates, point to a number of specific characteristics of the neighbourhoods which materially influenced the 'establishment' or collapse of associations following the end of the rebate dispute (Baldock, 1971). For example, he refers to a point made by Goetschius that the sheer size of estates may be a factor in the long-term fortunes of the tenants' associations. Goetschius noticed that of the seventy-five groups affiliated to the London Association of Housing Estates, the smallest estates that supported an organisation contained a minimum of 300 dwellings and the largest a maximum of 2000 (Goetschius, 1969, p. 4). These figures represent the limits of organisational viability, on the one hand providing a sufficiently large catchment population to support activities, and on the other a boundary beyond which identity is difficult to sustain and the organisational tasks become insurmountable. All the associations in Sheffield that collapsed in the immediate aftermath of the rent strike were much larger than Goetschius's maximum size. It seems likely that his figure can be exceeded for a short time during a period of particularly intense activity. Baldock also suggests that estates that did not have a tenants' hall or a suitable alternative were less capable of developing an 'established' organisation. Without a meeting place it is not possible to sustain a viable association. None of the pre-war estates had tenants' halls at the time of the rent rebate issue (although many were subsequently built). Baldock looked, in addition, at whether or not an alternative organisation providing social facilities existed on or near the estate. Community Associations or Workingmen's Clubs he argued, would dissipate one of the key roles of established tenants' associations. The older estates are well supplied with social clubs.

This is conditional upon the associations changing their functional emphasis, which is only marginally attributable to the presence or absence of a competing organisation. However, on the basis of a number of practical indices – the size of the estate, the existence of a hall and the existence or otherwise of social clubs – the pre-war estates were not favourably positioned to sustain a new organisation. The collapse of an issue-based association is likely to be triggered by these sorts of factors. But the factor that predicates their demise is the nature and type of social base. In 'traditional' working-class communities the characteristic response to collective crisis is one of instrumental solidarity. By the same token the fragmentary and less mature social systems of the post-war estates are more receptive to tenants' associations offering a broadly based range of social activities.

There are, however, countervailing factors to be taken into account with both the 'failed' and the 'established' associations. First, the pattern of disintegration of the organisations on older estates should *not* be read as the collapse of the social force of the estate. These areas are characterised by a high degree of associational spontaneity and informality. In short, it is almost certainly more difficult to rekindle militant political action from an established association with routine functions than from a social base with no formal organisation but with latent solidaristic instincts. It is precisely because the social bases of the post-war estates have weaker communal ties that they are more receptive to socially orientated tenants' associations. Second, it would be wrong to assert that these 'established' associations do not in some ways also represent the generalised interests of council house tenants albeit concealed in a different pattern and form of activity. This is essentially the same point made by Rex in his reading of immigrant and voluntary associations as agencies of 'incipient housing-classes-for-themselves' (Rex, 1973, p. 39). This, he argues, is particularly to be detected in the advocacy or 'trade union' role adopted by these organisations. All the tenants' associations that initially survived the rebate issue (80 per cent) played the roles indicated by Rex – social activity and pastoral care, welfare and bargaining action.

Although conflict is absorbed and institutionalised by the associations, they are simultaneously the partial expression of a conscious consumption interest akin to Rex and Moore's ideal-type housing classes. They represent the specific interest of council house tenants within the urban political system. Their mobilisation and life-cycles must be read against both the structure of the social system they are built on and the conception of the associational world as representing incipient consumption interests.

The most recent phase of the tenants' movement in Sheffield dates from 1978 and introduces new elements into the analysis. These involve the effects created by the early struggle and so represent a continuity of the movement in the city. It also fundamentally reflects the fact that the movement was defeated over the central issue of resisting changes to the rent structure. A decade on from the original dispute, its character and political strategies had undergone major revisions.

Effects of the 1968–9 tenants' movement

As argued in Chapter 2, the dominance of Labour's control of Sheffield city council and the virtual impossibility of pursuing single issues through party political channels was a major factor in the growth of the tenants' movement. It is within the Labour Party itself that some of the most enduring effects were created. The tenants' movement did not presage the victory of the political Left, as Ceccarelli argued in his analysis of Italian urban movements (as we have seen, Labour *lost* the 1968 local election in Sheffield). Nevertheless, a similar process of influence and responses to the tenants' movement had important consequences for the Labour Party in Sheffield.

But first of all it must be reiterated that the immediate objective of the tenants' movement to limit rent increases and to oppose the introduction of means-tested rebates was not successful. The 'lodger tax' was withdrawn by the Conservatives during their single year of office in the city (1968–9) but this was a small concession. They implemented a restructing of the rental system (causing some renewed protest action on the newer estates), raised the overall level of rents, and implemented a rebate scheme. By the time the campaign against the 'fair rent' Bill began two years later, council house rents were already, on a national basis, being brought to market levels. This represented an important step away from the notion of public housing as a general form of tenure within the housing system and towards the notion of public housing as a self-financing, residual or 'welfare' type of provision for families who could not afford owner occupancy. The Housing Finance Act (1972) consolidated this trend, and although there is evidence of wide-spread resistance to it in many parts of the country (Sklair, 1975) action was belated and unsuccessful in reversing the inexorable march towards fair rent public housing, underpinned by rebates for the poor.

It is clear that in Sheffield the struggle of 1968 to 1969 blunted the edge of the resistance to the Housing Finance Act. A new sympathy to the tenants' movement was apparent in the Labour Party at this period, born almost certainly of expediency in the wake of their electoral defeat in 1968. In addition, the focus of financial policy in housing had shifted to central government, and there was a growing recognition of this within the tenants' movement. Sheffield's own housing revenue account was also in a parlous state arising from debts incurred through the massive post-war building programme. For several years in the late 1960s and early 1970s all the rent collected from the entire city did not even cover the interest charges on the capital loans. It was here, in the face of the fiscal and political realities, that the tenants' movement had to accept its most complete defeat. The revived movement of the late 1970s does not seriously have housing finance and rent policy on its agenda. If it is to exist at all as an 'established' movement it is with the tacit acknowedgement of this basic fact.

The most immediate effect of the rent rebate dispute in

Sheffield was the defeat of Labour at the local elections in May 1968. Although this was set against a background of Labour's worst local government results since 1932–3, in the aftermath of the National Government debacle, it is doubtful whether Labour would have lost control of the city council had it not been for the rebate issue. The 'swing' of electoral support between the two main parties was strongly against Labour and was higher than the average for the city as a whole in wards with a high proportion of council houses. These normally safe Labour seats suddenly became very marginal as a result of the national and local components in the swing, and a number of them switched hands. The existence *per se* of tenants' associations on the estates may not have affected voting behaviour – the independent tenants' candidates did very poorly – but there was unquestionably an anti-Labour mood among council tenants that translated into abstentions and some switching to Conservative support.

The most enduring consequences of the tenants' movement of the late 1960s in Sheffield were to take place within the local Labour Party itself. After decades of election victories in which it had always been assumed that the council estates represented the bedrock of Labour's vote, it was dramatically clear that this support was not unconditional. This lesson underpins the current support for the new tenants' movement and the desire of the new and more youthful leadership of the Labour group to build their version of municipal socialism (Blunkett, interview in Boddy and Fudge 1984). During the rebate dispute the Labour Party was deeply divided on the attitude that should be taken to the tenants' movement. The ageing 'city fathers' followed a hard line against the supporters of the tenants, but in the aftermath of the election defeat their grip on power was weakened. A number of youthful councillors, among them the current leader, were first elected to the council in the early 1970s. Several councillors were nearly expelled from the party for espousing the cause of the tenants' movement. It is indicative of the changed balance of power from the mid-1970s that one of those councillors became leader of the Labour group following the resignation of Sir Ron Ironmonger, and another became leader of the South Yorkshire County Council. In many ways these events in Sheffield presaged developments that were to take place throughout the Labour Party nationally in the late 1970s; the resurgence of grassroots power and the growing importance of the accountability of elected representatives to their party branches. When David Blunkett, the current leader, came to power in 1980 he did so on a platform not only of inter-party accountability but of widening the decision-making process in the authority to include local government trade unions and groups within the wider community. This included active support for the new tenants' federation. A decade after the rent rebate dispute and in a period of very changed political and ideological perspectives towards council housing, enshrined in the 'right to buy' clauses of the 1980 Housing Act, the Labour Party in Sheffield now takes the tenants' movement to be one of its staunchest allies. The authority partly funds a full-time federation organiser, and a number of joint campaigns with the District and Constituency Labour Parties have made a significant impact. The Joint Campaign against the Sale of Council Houses ran for nearly two years in the early 1980s and has been partly instrumental in limiting sales of public housing in Sheffield. The Tenants' Federation also supported the council-sponsored 'Save our Buses' campaign and is currently involved in action against central control over local government finances and the abolition of the metropolitan counties.

The general process of the radicalisation of Sheffield Labour Party and the emergence of a leadership publicly espousing a form of municipal socialism was given significant impetus by the experience of electoral defeat in 1968. Although the tenants' movement was defeated on the central issue of means-tested rebates, the lessons of those years still echo through the local corridors of power; Labour's grassroots voters will not blindly follow a party establishment.

One rather more indirect consequence of the tenant's movement of 1968–9 was the development in the city of a large-scale community work service within the Family and Community Services Committee. David Blunkett, when he was chairman of the committee, encouraged this new departure (Baldock, 1982). It is particularly significant in the history of the tenants' movement because professional community workers have been largely instrumental in the revival of the movement in recent years. In the first place they helped establish a number of new tenant's associations, particularly on newer, smaller estates, and also revived some of the existing associations. Impetus was given to the need for a revived federal structure by the decision of the Housing Department to substitute the Housing Advisory Committee for a system of Area Consultative Committees. A number of community workers argued that this amounted to a divide and rule approach to the tenants' movement. All the known tenants' associations were subsequently invited to a meeting in early February 1978. Twenty-seven associations were represented, and from the meeting a steering committee was appointed to discuss the structure and functions of a new tenants' federation. Much of the discussion at this meeting concerned the past experiences of the tenants' movement. The minutes of the meeting recorded the following extract:

> Several members of the group had been involved in the Tenants' Co-ordinating Committee and more recently the Tenants' Consultative Committees. The disadvantages of these were seen in the former to be the emphasis on party politics and in the latter the Housing Department's attempt to split the organisation into smaller groups. It was felt important that this new organisation did not fail in a similar way.

It seems clear that the community workers played a key role in the early stages of the new federation by having the time and resources to undertake the administrative tasks, and, as Baldock observes 'the fact that community workers did not represent a political party probably did something to prevent destructive internal conflict' (Baldock, 1982, pp. 130–1). The involvement of employees of the authority in the new tenants' federation also paved the way for the rapid institutional acceptance of the movement. Initially the Housing Committee was sceptical about the revival of a centralised tenants' movement but in May 1978, only four months after the federation was re-established, a joint meeting between members of the Housing Committee and the federation met to discuss the extent and nature of the participaton of tenants in the policy-making structure. The Housing Advisory Committee was revived as a joint consultative body and federation representatives joined a number of standing committees – on heating, the modernisation programme and a working group considering the terms of tenancy agreements under the Tenants' Charter. Community workers thus paved the way for the new federation by helping to build and sustain individual associations, initiating the early city-wide liaison meetings, providing the framework in which some of the mistakes of the past could be remedied, and by being agents for institutional dialogue.

But whatever the basis on which the new Sheffield Federation of Tenants' and Residents' Associations has been established, it is absolutely clear that an historic compromise has been made. The rents issue is no longer seriously part of the movement's agenda and the tacit alliance between Sheffield's ruling Labour Party and the new federation could hardly be further from the militant, anti-Labour protest movement of 1967 to 1969.

The two major tactical problems that ultimately confronted the tenants' movement in Sheffield in 1969 were how to sustain a rent strike and how to hold a loose federation of individual associations together as a political force. Both these questions were cross-cut by a third important element: the attitude of the political Left to tenants' action. As we saw in Chapter 2, the interlinking of urban issues with the wider working-class movement was the acid test for Castells in the evolution of, as he saw them, correctly conceived and defined 'urban social movements'. We saw that his own evidence did not support his prognosis and that in his recent phase Castells re-writes the relationships and conditions that lead to the creation of urban social movements, including an assertion of the autonomy of urban movements from political parties. The evidence from the record of the Sheffield tenants' movement suggests that both Castells's 'early' and 'late' formulations are incongruous in the British context, although the plea for autonomy may in the long run be valid. The strategies available to the tenants' movement in this country create major obstacles to independently generated political change.

Political strategies of the tenants' movement

Whatever else it achieved, the tenants' movement in Sheffield in the late 1960s did not stop the restructuring of rents and the introduction of means-tested rebates. Moorhouse *et al.* are plain wrong when they argue that, 'Rent strikes have been of great importance to the working class as a whole in forcing reluctant governments into action in the field of housing, *most notably to control the operation of market forces in the determination of rents*' (Moorhouse, Wilson and Chamberlain, 1972, p. 150, emphasis added). The only example in the British context that can be quoted with any justification to support such a claim is the famous rent strike of private tenants in the special circumstances of Glasgow in 1915. But there are no examples in the modern period, or even the era of council house tenants' movements, that rent strikes caused anything other than a localised impact. Hampton's assessment is certainly more accurate: 'The spontaneous eruption of feeling that can shake a city council is not a noticeable influence on national housing policy' (Hampton, 1970, p. 273). Most of the evidence indicates that the rent strike as a political tactic is extremely difficult to enforce and frequently ends in disarray and confusion.

In Sheffield the rent strike was finally called for when the Labour group of councillors decided by a narrow majority to implement the rebate scheme. At the time a majority of tenants' associations around the city supported this move. The atmosphere was angry and militant, although a number of tenants' leaders took their associations into the strike very reluctantly. Fear of going into debt is deeply ingrained in 'respectable' working-class culture and is a strong countervailing influence to the solidaristic response to a commonly experienced injustice. The transfer of the strike tactic from the industrial to the residential sphere confronts this basic problem. In the industrial context strikes are much more directly effective because they are usually implemented and sustained by established and tested workplace representative organisations with years of experience and day-to-day knowledge of the likely responses of their members and the employers. There is a somewhat parlous but nevertheless established place for industrial strikes in law. None of these conditions – visible collective action, organisational support systems, legal recognition – can be transferred to the residential context. Rent strikes are vulnerable because ultimately they depend on individuals in their own homes breaching tenancy agreements. The threat of eviction is a card that local authorities are quick to play. Large numbers of tenants fall into rent arrears because of low incomes, but the conscious act of withholding rent for a political purpose is on a different plane of consciousness, and may indeed aggravate long-term problems with rent payments. In the Sheffield strike the problem of determining precisely who was withholding rent rather than those who said they were withholding was a major factor in the decision of some associations to split from the federation and call off the rent strike. On the other estates a token number of people maintained the strike but within weeks this action also petered out.

Given these factors it is also difficult to sustain the claim that rent strikes 'represent a clear form of class struggle – property owners versus propertyless' (Moorhouse *et al.*, 1972, p. 151). There is confusion in this view, partly arising from the longstanding debate about the ownership of residential property in class formation, but primarily in this context because it fails to distinguish between the roles played by public and private landlords. As will be shown in the next chapter, this sectoral divide has important repercussions on the structuring and outcomes of urban protest. The fact is that in Sheffield the rent strike was against a municipal authority controlled for over half a century by the traditional party of the British working class.

Castells's perspectives and the Sheffield tenants' movement

Castells's fluctuating perspectives on the political role of urban social movements does not at any stage fully account for these factors. First, in relation to his phase one position, it is not the case in the British context that urban conflict – powerfully expressed in the tenants' movement – became a major 'conjuncture' for social transformation. Rather, the history of the public sector tenants' movement should be read as a defensive reaction by a working-class social base against an apparently hostile outside world. From the mid-1960s the movement fought against attempts to incorporate gradually the council house stock into the market system, through market level rents and the right to buy. Despite its remarkable history and some local successes, on most occasions the tenants' movement has not succeeded, and the tasks established by Castells for fully fledged urban social movements have been outside the terms of the movement's activity. Neither is Castells's notion of 'pluriclassism' of any relevance in this context. The council house tenants' movement was and remains rigidly locked into its manual worker, public sector social base and did not link at any stage either to private sector tenants or to the owner occupiers. What happened in Sheffield was not political class struggle but a form of political action based on the consumption interests of public tenants which was, to some extent, structured by a class-defined social milieu.

There is also a sense in which the tenants' movement in Sheffield in the late 1960s was not allowed to become part of the political class struggle. This point contradicts Castells's phase one notion of the links with the wider Labour movement, particularly its 'vanguard' sections, if urban social movements are to make a sustained political impact. Important contact was made between the tenants' movement and the Left parties and sects and the trade union movement in Sheffield, but the impact of the relationship was generally divisive. As we saw in Chapter 2, Castells himself has now renounced his earlier perspectives, largely because his empirical work failed to support his prognosis. He does not, however, re-analyse his case studies but moves uncritically into his phase three position in which he argues that urban movements must be autonomous from other political parties or political organisations. But this leap is not adequately grounded in empirical analysis (as we saw, the crucial case study of the Madrid Citizens' Movement is badly flawed in this respect). Castells fails, therefore, to discuss the *nature* of the linkages between urban social movements and the wider working-class movement, offering only blunt 'autonomy' as his new option. The experience in Sheffield does suggest, however, a range of problems in the politicisation of the tenants' movement.

The major point is that the Left groups and the trade unions failed to understand the essentially spontaneous nature of the tenants' movement. The movement originated within the female-dominated neighbourhood networks on some pre-war estates. The role of women in rent strike activity has been observed on several occasions, notably in the 1915 Glasgow incident. Responsibility for rent payments, even in normal times, often falls within the archetypal role of women in some types of working-class community. This combination of factors accounts for the crucial influence of women in the initial stages of the rent rebate controversy in Sheffield, although the organisational experience that was quickly fed into the incipient tenants' movement was predominately trade union-based – male and committee dominated. The trade union model fitted uncomfortably into the less structured mode of organisation that was characteristic of the first and spontaneously generated tenants' associations. The clash between these approaches was a pervasive theme during the formative period of the tenants' movement.

As the movement gathered pace, the intervention of the Communist Party made a significant contribution to the spread of associations across the city. They had their own network and many communist members were themselves council tenants. As we have seen, their activity, inflamed by a hostile local press, led to a split in the tenants' federation. Despite their contribution to the development of new associations, their political purpose was primarily centred on building support for their own organisation rather than in sustaining an autonomous tenants' movement. Ultimately there proved to be an incompatibility in these dual roles which created confusion and divisions among the tenants. A second political faction, a small group of International Socialists (now the Socialist Workers' Party) based at Sheffield University, made early links with the tenants' movement in an attempt to introduce a political line into the struggle. Essentially this consisted of an opportunistic platform of support for the tenants against the intrusion of the Labour and Communist Parties while trying to harness the movement to their own anti-capitalist programme. It was a short-lived and unfruitful association that hinged on one or two personalities.

Although the Left tried to 'raise the political level' of the tenants' movement, they found urban protest an unfamiliar and difficult terrain that did not easily conform to their workplace and trade union-centred experience. They did not consciously seek to create 'urban social movements' in Castells's original sense of the phrase, but these *were* the conditions under which urban protest must theoretically have been ripe for harnessing to the 'wider working-class movement'. Not only did this attempt fail, but it positively damaged the solidarity of the tenants' movement at a critical stage of the struggle. The post-1978 tenants' movement is not a mass movement, as we have seen, but is akin to Castells's middle phase position (the broad Left strategy). It was argued in Chapter 1 that this phase was distinctive because the emphasis shifted away from the crucial role of urban social movements as initiators of social transformation. Instead these movements were harnessed into the drive of the Left forces to win an electoral power base. This is Castells's most useful reading of urban politics in relation to the British situation. His position is achieved, however, only by downgrading the role of urban social movements, and his more recent perspective moves the argument away from the idea of political alliances. But the idea of a 'local socialism' (Boddy and Fudge, 1984), based on links between the Labour Party, public sector trade unions, and community organisations and movements, marks an important development in urban politics in this country.

The question remains whether Castells's phase three position is any better as a basis for analysing urban movements in Britain. It will be recalled that in Chapter 2 considerable doubt was expressed about the empirical validity of his major case study – of the Madrid Citizens' Movement – and whether his claim to have identified a fully formed urban social movement was justified. These movements must contain three core characteristics, according to Castells: involvement in issues of collective consumption, concern with questions of cultural identity, and struggling for local self-control over services. Moreover, they must be fully autonomous from the influence of other political bodies, especially political parties. Only then is an urban social movement capable of effecting a change in urban meaning. But Castells gives no unequivocal guidelines for showing how urban social movements in practice intervene in the political process, while insisting on their autonomous status. In the British context, however, this interface between the movement and between the local authority (which is the dominant force in all local political systems) is the crucial strategic terrain. It determines their tactics and is very influential in establishing their organisational characteristics. For some groups insider contacts are important, but for most urban movements, outside the conventional interest group world, the problem is how and on what terms to establish a bargaining relationship with the local council. For some organisations and social interests this is an insurmountable problem because they are systematically excluded from developing a negotiating position. Castells still does not confront the important questions of non-decision and exclusion.

Castells's three core elements – of collective consumption, cultural identity and local control – represent a crystallisation of experience drawn from a global analysis of urban movements, and at a theoretical level may be thought of as providing an ideal-type of urban social movements. As with the original notion of collective consumption, much further refinement of the model is a prerequisite to making it analytically functional. The theme of collective consumption is, of course, central to the discussion of the tenants' movement. The theme of cultural identity, of freely chosen sociocultural milieux, is less obviously useful in this context. It would not, of itself, have led us to examine the social base characteristics of the estates and their local systems, which are crucial to understanding the patterns of establishment and disestablishment of the associations. The cultural context of council house estates is solidaristic but within a parochial and limiting 'subordinate' value system, to return to Parkin's phrase. The theme of local self-control is also only partially expressed in the incipient consumption interests represented through the tenants' associations (even in their 'established' and socially orientated idiom). The ideal of tenant control over housing policy was implicit in the rent struggles of the late 1960s and early 1970s. The suggestion of a Tenants' Charter (found, for example, in the Labour government's housing Green Paper of 1977) also incorporates a limited extension of tenants' rights and by implication control over some aspects of estate management. But this must be seen as a reaction to the bureaucratic administrative procedures that surround public sector housing. In the 1980 Housing Act the idea of a Tenants' Charter was effectively dropped in favour of the right to buy, portrayed by the Conservative government as the ultimate in tenants' rights. This is a good example of what Castells means when he talks about the competition for urban meaning; in this case between council housing as 'use-value' (for need) or as 'exchange value' (as a commodity). But the theme of local self-management and the control of urban services as it is presented in *The City and the Grassroots* is far ahead of the limited issues fought, and lost, by the British tenants' movement.

The Sheffield tenants' movement, judged by the three core elements and the assertion of political autonomy, is certainly not an urban social movement of the Castells variety. As has been argued, neither does Castells's own case study of the Citizens' Movement in Madrid fit readily into the model. Both movements conform more closely to the category of organisation referred to by Castells as 'collective consumption trade unions'. Here groups organise over urban issues as a result of the failure of the Labour movement to take up the issue; but these organisations never broaden the basis of their activity to insist on or provoke a change of urban meaning. This is the same context in which Castells locates the 1915 Glasgow Rent Strike – as a struggle to defend or establish 'use-value' in the capitalist urban system. The strategy for achieving this in the 1980s is more akin, however, to his phase two position, as we argued earlier in the chapter. The notion of local socialism is essentially about defending an 'urban meaning' based on use-value – on the defence and extension of public services for need. The tenants' movement in Sheffield is part of the alliance of forces involved. Given the defeats of the past and the tactical problems of organising a militant tenants' movement, this may be the most fruitful way forward. But the movement is no longer independent and is very scaled down in size. It may be that far from representing one wing of a new municipal socialism, we have, in fact, witnessed a process of subtle incorporation and de-politicisation of the spontaneous mass movement of the 1960s and early 1970s. In this sense perhaps Castells is right to insist on political autonomy. Given the distinctive characteristics of the council house tenants' social base it may be that if the movement, in the words of Castells, is 'to come again' as an urban social movement, it will not be from the committee rooms of the broad Left but from within the neighbourhood networks of the estates themselves.

Chapter 5

Ideologies in Local Politics – The Ratepayers' and Squatters' Movements

Castells's early exploration of the ideologies surrounding the conventional urbanism thesis was pathfinding, and led to the opening up of the whole field of urban studies based on collective consumption. But in his concern with urban social movements Castells does not systematically explore the influence of ideology on social movement formation. The possibility of important effects on the genesis and types of urban movements arising out of social system ideologies was discussed in Chapter 3. It was argued that ideology was one of three major formative influences on the nature of urban political organisations in Britain, the others being the structure of the local political system and social base characteristics. In the case study on the council house tenants' movement in Chapter 4, attention focused on tactical and strategic issues within the local political system, and on the influence of social base characteristics on the life-cycles of the associations. This chapter is concerned with the third element in the analytical field: to illustrate how ideology operates in the practice of two distinct urban movements. There is a gap in Castells's analytical method on this issue, and the material here is designed to show why it is an important omission.

The two types of organisation chosen are ratepayers' associations and squatters' movements. The choice of these groups is to juxtapose a 'right-wing' movement with a 'radical' movement, to show that urban social movements span the political spectrum. But primarily the choice has been made to illustrate how property-based ideologies can surface in a number of guises. The ratepayers' movement operates within the dominant value-system of free enterprise and the primacy of private property; the squatters challenge the ideologies of ownership of domestic property both in the public and private sectors and seek 'alternative' methods of access and allocation to housing. The two sets of organisations occupy, therefore, the same ideological terrain but stand in an entirely contrasting relationship to it. The limited records of their activity that exist also suggest contrasts in the way that the public/private sector ideology influences and works through them, generally implying a critique of public services and an institutionalised defence of the private sector. The existence and pattern of activity of these organisations offers, therefore, an opportunity to make a comparative assessment of the operation of specific ideologies in the formation and strategies of two types of urban social movement.

Both sets of organisations were very active in the 1970s and have 'declined' in recent years. But as argued earlier in the book, noting the lull does nothing to explain the social forces represented by urban social movements or the process of mobilisation. These imply understanding the patterns of disestablishment, absorption and co-optation, and the directions in which the social forces they represent are subsequently channelled. Once again the important theme of the influence of the party political system on the deployment and tactics of urban protest organisations is prominent, particularly in the case of the ratepayers' associations.

The case study presentation follows the same pattern as the previous chapter: a brief review of the recent history of the movement across the country as a whole is followed by more detailed examples that highlight and describe key themes. The ratepayer case study is based on original research by the author in the Barnsley area of South Yorkshire; the material on the squatters' movement is drawn from a number of recent research documents and publications.

The ratepayers' movement

Ratepayer movements are relatively unexplored in the local politics literature and are referred to either in the context of election studies (Sharpe, 1967) or narrative accounts of 'middle-class' politics (King and Nugent, 1978; Nugent, 1979). Most of the studies are of long-standing organisations in the pre-1974 local political system. These associations do not form a unified or coherent movement and are characterised as parochial and idiosyncratic. Under the conditions of high levels of inflation and the major reorganisation of local government which took place in 1973–4, a new wave of militant ratepayer associations emerged in all parts of the country, particularly in the Labour-dominated areas of the North of England, the Midlands and South Wales. In most cases these groups opted to fight in the local electoral arena. A clear majority affiliated to the newly established National Association of Ratepayers' Action Groups (formed in June 1974) rather than the moderate National Union of Ratepayer Associations (established since 1921) which drew its membership from the older associations.

Of the pre-1974 associations a large number, particularly in the 1950s, took the form of 'concealed' Conservatives (Grant, 1977; Nugent, 1979), running candidates with the tacit and uncontested approval of the local Conservative Associations. However, the tendency in the 1960s and 1970s was for these groups gradually to be absorbed into the national Conservative movement. Richards describes a typical concealed Conservative ratepayer organisation in his analysis of politics in Southampton. In the period between 1934 and 1954 control of the council oscillated between Labour and Ratepayer, but thereafter the Conservative-Ratepayer alignment became more explicit, mainly on the grounds of organisational expediency (Richards, 1967). Links between ratepayer groups and the major national parties are not confined only to the Conservatives. In Manchester, for example, Bulpitt describes the close association between the Liberal Party and the ratepayer organisations; a Liberal councillor was chairman of the Manchester Ratepayers' Council (Bulpitt, 1967). In Barnsley in the early 1980s some of the leading ratepayer personalities and councillors joined the SDP.

Beyond this range of 'concealed national parties' (Grant, 1977) or activists who adopted a ratepayer label for tactical reasons, pre-1974 ratepayer organisations are eclectic. Grant describes a ratepayers' association based in the resort area of Seaton in Devon. Here retired newcomers mainly from professional backgrounds sustained a group to preserve the town from commercialisation and to curtail rates expenditure. He describes this organisation as a 'genuine local party' in that it stands outside nationally structured politics and is focused on the specific interests of one local population (Grant, 1977, pp. 77–83). But this political formation does draw heavily on the pervasive public/private sector ideologies, with their implicit critique of rate-sponsored public service provision. This can be seen more clearly in Stanyer's account of a ratepayer movement in Exeter in the early 1960s, when the group won a number of council seats on a specifically anti-rates/anti-public spending platform. This example also highlights two of the classic propositions of ratepayer politics: their claim to be non-political (by which they in fact mean non-*party* political) and the strongly populist claim to be the 'watchdogs of the ratepayers' (over local spending decisions) (Stanyer, 1967). A large number of anti-Labour organisations existed in areas of Labour domination of local politics where the Conservatives were weak or made no systematic intervention into local government affairs. These groups often called themselves Ratepayers but in other areas the same types of organisation were called 'Citizens', 'Residents' or simply 'Independents'. Additionally, some ratepayer groups, often not competing in local elections, base their existence not specifically on the rates question but on a range of local environmental or planning issues. Nugent cites the example of the Jesmond and District Household and Ratepayers' Association, which 'only rarely concerned itself with rates as such. Its main interests were environmental and community issues' (Nugent, 1979, p. 27).

Before 1974, as these examples suggest, the ratepayer movement was a fragmented and disparate force, important in some localities where ratepayer associations controlled local councils, ephemeral in other areas where they did not compete in elections but acted as conventional pressure groups. But it would be wrong to draw the boundary between the pre- and post-1974 ratepayer movements too sharply. Many of the key elements of the political programme of ratepayer politics can be detected, to varying degrees, across the different types of organisation. These are framed around two ideologies that partially structure the local political environment – the ratepayer ideology and the public/private sector ideolgies around the provision of the urban public services. The universality of these ideologies finds concrete expression in the election manifestos and policy documents commonly published by ratepayer movements within (although not exclusively) the electoral area. This is the case despite their parochial milieu and tenuous interlinking at the national level. The archetypal position is based on hostility towards the rating system, with frequent demands for their abolition, opposition to rate increases and opposition to party politics in local government. The extended demands usually include antipathy towards interventionist land-use planning and welfare services (often described as 'luxuries') frequent and generalised accusations of inefficiency and overspending by local authorities, support for the sale of council houses as a means of enhancing the property-owning democracy, for increasing spending on law and order and for an extension of the private market and competitive tendering for the provision of public services. This general defence of what is said to be the "ratepayers' interest" is informed by a neo-liberal economics and is often overlaid by a strongly populist appeal; the talk is of what will happen when 'we the people' take charge of council affairs. Not all the organisations share all these ideas but they are the major themes of mainstream ratepayer politics and they are generated by the existence of universal local political ideology.

In all the more recent studies of ratepayer politics these organisations are characterised as ephemeral to mainstream local political systems and are described as an overwhelmingly middle-class phenomenon (Grant, 1977; King and Nugent, 1978; Nugent, 1979). The significance of the ratepayer movement is spoken of mainly as a conservative influence on the minds of local politicians in relation to budgeting. Grant suggests that 'their greatest impact is through the influence that their existence (or even the possibility of their existence) exerts on the minds of councillors' (Grant, 1977, p. 102). But an assessment of social movements that is restricted to narrative accounts and descriptions of the conditions under which they develop, although necessary, does not properly locate their significance. They are not a surface phenomenon but are one form of expression of the fundamental ideologies of local politics. From this standpoint a re-assessment of the social base from which ratepayer movements draw their support, particularly in the post-1974 phase, also needs to be made. Their support base is not 'wholly' or 'overwhelmingly' middle class but should be more precisely related to consumption factors, especially home ownership, which cut across the social class spectrum. Saunders, for example, has found important evidence of support for an anti-rates political programme among home-owners and that this is more strongly associated with manual worker owner/occupiers than with home-owners who are from the non-manual and professional occupational categories (Saunders, 1982, pp. 8–10).

There is, additionally, an historical basis for this sectoral division that closely aligns with the ratepayer movement's anti-party politics critique, which often conceals a strongly anti-Labour party perspective. This is a vestige of the response to the rise of Labour in municipal politics in the early part of this century. It has led some ratepayer groups to the contradictory position of seeking a power base in the council chambers specifically to challenge Labour while disavowing the notion of party politics in local government. This may be read as a nineteenth-century throwback when an explicit association was made between property ownership and the local franchise; this was statutorily enshrined in the Municipal Corporation Act of 1835 and only reluctantly conceded to universal suffrage at the end of the century. The rise of Labour heightened local conflict, particularly over the rates issue, into an explicitly anti-party stance on the basis that property and not a free franchise is the source of citizenship. Recently such a notion has been openly supported by business interests who complain that their rate contributions are disproportionately high in relation to domestic ratepayers. The growth of extensive programmes of council housing associated with Labour-controlled local authorities, and the spread of home ownership, both from the mid-1920s onwards, have tended to polarise further the political effects of ownership and non-ownership, and is at the root of Dunleavy's specification of a 'ratepayer ideology' which differentiates council house tenants and owner occupiers on the basis of degree of subsidisation and rate-paying (see Chapter 3).

These themes, of the ideological structuring of local politics, the role of party politics in determining the conditions for the emergence of a specific type of urban social movement, and the significance of consumption factors in creating the social base of support, are all exemplified in the case of a large and sustained ratepayer movement inaugurated in the Metropolitan District of Barnsley in June 1974.

Barnsley Ratepayers' Association

The ratepayer movement in Barnsley was part of the new generation of militant associations that sprang up all over the country in the period 1973 to 1975. The impact of inflation in the economy, but particularly the consequences of local government reform, produced a very high level of rate increases in the new Barnsley Metropolitan District. The expanded authority inherited extensive debts from its constituent parts – the old Barnsley borough and a large number of urban and rural district councils formerly in the old West Riding of Yorkshire. The Ratepayers' Association was formed with the specific intention of fighting for seats on the local council. From its inception the association sustained a reasonable electoral performance, winning seats in former Labour strongholds, ousting leading Labour politicians and winning a steady 30 per cent share of the vote in the local elections between 1975 and 1982. What accounts for this rapid growth and persistence in an area that is among the top half dozen most solidly Labour supporting areas in the country?

In his study, Grant suggests four pre-conditions for the successful establishment of ratepayer organisations in the post-1974 local government system: a widespread feeling of hostility towards party politics in local government, a weak Conservative Party in the local political system, hostility towards the rating system, and high rate increases (Grant, 1977). While these pre-conditions were all present in Barnsley, they were also present in other areas of South Yorkshire and elsewhere where ratepayer organisations have not been successful. There must be other factors at work. Grant also suggests that in the re-organised local government system ratepayer activity will be 'ephemeral' because indignation against rate increases will quickly evaporate and because local conflicts in small urban districts will disappear as a result of the restructuring of the boundaries. In fact, one of the special conditions in Barnsley that underpinned the success of the ratepayer movement was the scale of restructuring of the administrative boundaries. Although their recent performance has been less good, their record over a period of eight years put them at the heart of politics in the district. A social force based on an issue as ingrained into the ideological fabric of local government as the rates seems unlikely to dissolve because of administrative restructuring. The unpopularity of party politics in local government may have been enhanced by the situation, after 1974, in which local government became more party-dominated. Presumably the unpopularity of the rates did not end with the 1974 reform. Local political environments are ideologically structured. Particular ideologies favourably condition the circumstances for new political groupings to emerge, but equally showing how that energy can be dissipated or channelled elsewhere.

Only a brief assessment of the organisational form and structure adopted by the ratepayer movement is necessary because the mode or organisation is relatively conventional. The Barnsley association is almost wholly geared towards running candidates in the local elections and is loosely based on electoral wards. The critique that they mounted was potent because they challenged both the legitimacy of party politics in local government and, specifically, the political style and historical precedence of the Labour Party itself. They argued that despite (indeed, because of) the powerful electoral base the ruling Labour Party machine is oligarchic and, second, because the rise of Labour is synonymous with a period of expansion in local authority services, the legitimacy of a party dominated local government system is questioned.

In order to locate this argument and the point at which the ratepayers intervened, it is useful to document briefly the historical role of Labour in Barnsley politics. Attention then focuses on the specific conditions in the mid-1970s that acted as the catalyst to the formation of the ratepayer movement.

The rise of Labour

Barnsley claims early fame in the annals of local politics by having the first working man elected as a local councillor. John Normansell served on the borough council in 1872 with the financial backing of the Yorkshire Miners' Association (YMA). However, the local Labour movement remained in the shadow of Lib-Labism until after the First World War. The YMA, for example, continued to support the town's Liberal MP, Joseph Walton, a colliery owner, until he retired in 1922. In 1918, however, the Trades Council and the Labour Party merged into a formal alliance with the specific intention of fighting the local elections on an independent basis. This they did in 1919, and as early as 1921 temporarily won a majority on the council by voting as a bloc in the aldermanic elections against a fragmented group of Liberals, Independents and Conservatives. Labour quickly assumed control of the Board of Guardians and began their continuous control of Barnsley Council in 1927, interrupted for only a few years in the early 1930s as a consequence of the events surrounding the National Government debacle.

The organisational initiatives for these early campaigns came from a small group of local leaders with political bases in the miners' union and in the powerful shopworkers' union in the Co-op. These leaders held enormous powers of patronage in a party machine that was by no means as strong as its electoral support might suggest; but the commitment to ameliorating the appalling social conditions of the town quickly enabled them to outflank the old Victorian and Edwardian caucuses. Through the inter-war period and into the 1950s, the names of Sheerian, McVie (from Barnsley Trades Council) and Jones and Wright (from the YMA) recur in the political history of Barnsley. Edward Sheerian was undoubtedly the leading operator behind the scenes by virtue of his remarkable tenure of office as secretary of Barnsley Trades Council and Labour Party between 1918 and 1953. And because the calibre of the Labour concillors was not high, the party evolved a highly authoritarian style.

After the Second World War the ageing leadership was increasingly challenged by a new generation of activists drawn mainly from the Labour League of Youth. New pressures from expanding service provision and boundary extensions compounded the internal political problems facing the founding fathers; but when the time came the political succession was well organised. At the ballot box Labour's position was impregnable. Even through the period of massive anti-Labour swings in 1967 and 1968, which toppled Labour's control of the Sheffield council, Barnsley Labour Party lost only one seat to the 'Citizens' (the belatedly formed alliance in 1935 of anti-Labour groups) and one to a Liberal. In the 1973 elections for the new sixty-seat Metropolitan District Council, Labour won fifty-four seats. But this overwhelming electoral strength concealed a party machine that was fragile. For example, in 1970 at the constituency level (where individual party membership is registered), Barnsley Labour Party had a total individual membership of only 159, whereas the parliamentary member, Roy Mason, had a majority of over 20,000 in the general election of that year. The leaders at the centre of political power presided over an organisational shell.

The ratepayers' campaign

When the Ratepayers' Association began its campaign in 1974, it singled out for special attack the weakness of the Labour Party organisation compared with its strength of control over the local council. Their critique was particularly directed at Labour's historical domination of the town hall. The association between the rise of the Labour Party and the period of rapid expansion in local authority service provision is a close one. In the hands of the ratepayer pamphleteers this relationship became a double-edged sword, on the one hand as the reason for profligate spending (and too high rates), and on the other as the justification for their view that local government should be free of party politics. For Labour the impression of an imperious and unaccountable oligarchy in control of the town hall was difficult to dispel, even though historically and institutionally the link between party and local authority is complex and not necessarily contingent. The fragility of Labour's party organisation compared to the strength of its control was a major sustaining factor in the ratepayer movement in Barnsley.

The Association was formed following a well orchestrated campaign by a local businessman and night-club owner who, at the time, also held the important position of Secretary of the National Association of Ratepayer Action Groups. Large rate increases in 1974 of up to 100 per cent in some cases provided extremely fertile political conditions. These were due to deficits inherited from the pre-1973 authorities, but also from the decision to make Barnsley rather than Sheffield the centre of the new Metropolitan County of South Yorkshire, involving an expensive town centre office development.

The Labour leaders were duped into attending a public

meeting organised by ratepayer activists at the 'Ba Ba' night-club where six hundred people came to hear explanations for the rate increases. They were received very badly. The meeting was given full-page coverage in the local press and the demand to establish a Ratepayers' Association was prominently featured. 'All the people who voted Citizen or Liberal in the local elections and the 16,000 who voted Conservative in the General Election do not have a representative between them' (*Barnsley Chronicle*, June 1974). A number of area branches were subsequently formed, loosely based on electoral wards and under the overall direction of the Barnsley and District Ratepayers' Association. The activists in the organisation at this time were mainly self-employed small businessmen and middle-management grade engineers. The suspicion of middle-class self-interest spurred the Labour Party into collecting a file of information about the leading Ratepayers' Association members. The revelation of this in the local press provided headline news for several weeks: 'Secret Dossier Being Collected!', 'Is Big Brother in Barnsley?!' Publicity of this sort gave impetus to the campaign themes that emerged for the 1975 local elections; the idea that Big Brother is not only alive and well in Barnsley but is a profiligate spender of ratepayers' money.

When the Ratepayer election manifesto was published it contained a 'twenty-five point plan' which emphasised the need to eliminate 'waste' from local authority spending. The text made the startling claim that, 'If we can direct all waste into proper channels, the rates we pay could be eliminated'. Priority was given to scrutinising councillors' expenses, curtailing the size of committees, examining the efficency of officers, and to the abolition of departments that were losing money. A particular dislike was expressed for the Planning and Direct Works Departments. A policy of transferring the education service to the national purse was adopted in the plan. It was proposed to spend more on the police. In subsequent years the political programme developed a strongly populist appeal, describing what would happen when 'We, the people, gain control of the Council', or warning against the menace of party politics in local affairs. The message of 'People, Not Party Politics' was highlighted in all their election addresses and always closely linked to the 'extravagance' and 'waste' imposed by the Labour

Party. The 1978 manifesto reproduced the famous Kitchener poster from the First World War, but now urging a Ratepayer vote under the slogan 'People Not Politics'.

Their performance in the local elections was far superior to any of the opposition organisations in the post-war years. In Table 5.1, the figures in the brackets show the share of the vote for each party in the wards they contested. The figure in the adjacent column is the number of contests each party fought. A number of seats were uncontested.

TABLE 5.1   *Percentage share of the vote for each party, Barnsley 1975–81*

	Labour		Ratepayer		Conservative		Liberal		Other
1975	43.8	19	27.9	14	7.8	11	15.7	9	5.3
			(37.9)		(13.5)		(33.2)		
1976	49.1	20	30.7	18	5.3	8	10.4	6	3.6
			(34.1)		(13.4)		(34.6)		
1977*	50.3	19	21.2	11	19.6	19	4.2	3	4.6
			(36.6)		(9.6)		(26.6)		
1978	51.8	18	32.9	15	8.5	8	3.5	3	3.3
			(39.5)		(19.0)		(20.8)		
1979	56.2	66	28.6	39	6.6	12	3.8	6	4.8
			-		-		-		
1980	64.6	17	29.7	16	3.9	8	1.5	2	0.5
			(31.5)		(8.2)		(13.1)		
1981*	60.2	16	21.2	9	10.0	10	1.1	5	0.8
			(37.4)		(16.0)		(17.6)		
1975–81	53.7	100%	27.4	76%	8.8	59%	5.7	26%	3.3
	(53.7)		(36.2)		(13.3)		(24.3)		

* County council election

1979 was an all-out election. The figures represent the share of votes cast and not the poll, because each voter has a choice of casting up to three votes.

The table shows Ratepayer candidates winning an average of 27 per cent of the total poll between 1975 and 1981 and over 36 per cent in the wards they contested. They had candidates in three-quarters of the wards in that period. At the first single candidate elections in the Metropolitan District (1975) the newly formed Ratepayers' Association won six seats and ousted in the process both the leader and deputy leader of the Labour group of councillors. By 1979 they had built their representation on the council to fourteen seats. But in 1980, a very good year nationally for Labour, they lost six seats (and gained one), although the Ratepayers' share of the vote held up well compared to the swing against the Conservatives across the country and in the District itself.

What was the basis of this sustained pattern of support? The opportunity to vote for a viable alternative to Labour clearly brought out a large number of electors who did not normally take part in local elections. But the initial upsurge of support cannot be accounted for by that factor. The principal factors involved concern over the consequences of the local government reform that took effect in 1974 and the link between the ratepayer ideology and the pattern of housing tenure in the area.

Local government reform

Local government reform in 1974 brought together fourteen separate areas to make up the Metropolitan District of Barnsley – the old Barnsley Borough and Urban and Rural Districts formerly in the West Riding of Yorkshire. Although an appropriate geographical unit in the context of the new South Yorkshire County Council, the new District was one of the most fragmented authorities to emerge from the boundary revisions under the 1972 Local Government Act. Areas with many decades of quite separate political traditions and practices, and different personalities, were thrown into a metropolitan scale of administration and political organisation that was alien. The organisational position of the Labour Party, which had branches spread throughout the area (albeit with their own traditions) ensured them a dominant position on the new District Council, taking in 1973 90 per cent of the seats in the first elections in the new authorities. The anti-Labour groupings and Independents, who had an important place in the political history of the West Riding councils, were completely swamped. The largest group, the 'Citizens', won only a few seats in the old borough where their support was traditionally concentrated.

They had no political base in the outlying urban and rural districts and were unable to face the challenge of building an organisation outside their stronghold areas. In short, the anti-Labour forces, isolated in their small enclaves within a new and vastly bigger structure, collapsed in the face of a much better equipped and more adaptable Labour Party machine.

Across the District as a whole, a political vacuum had been created by the decimation of the opposition groups, and it was this void that the ratepayers' movement exploited in the elections in 1975 and subsequently. They performed best in the areas formerly held by the Citizens, but have consistently held a strong position in the outlying semi-rural wards in which the pre-1974 councils were strongly influenced by Independents and the Labour Party itself. Some of the Independent councillors joined the Ratepayers and have drawn votes to the new anti-Labour organisation as a result; but much of the support for the Ratepayers in these areas is a consequence of a strong parochial attachment by many voters to the organisations and traditions of the old urban and rural districts. There is a feeling of resentment against the political domination of the new District Council by 'Barnsley'. The old borough is by far the biggest and most powerful element, and all the main leaders on the council are politicians from the borough Labour Party. A resentment vote against the functional and political domination of Barnsley has been an important factor in the pattern of support for the Ratepayers in these outlying wards. It plays not only on the parochialism and attachment to more immediate and localised councils, but also fits neatly into the ideological perception within the ratepayer programme of an overbearing, bureaucratic and centralised authority at the heart of local government. Whether this reaction continues as people become more familiar with the new institutional forms remains to be seen.

A more pervasive factor that sustains the Ratepayer candidates is the spatial arrangement in the District of the housing tenure categories. The differential perception within the ratepayer ideology between council house tenants (non-ratepayers/subsidised) and owner occupiers (ratepayers/unsubsidised) predicts a concentration of support for the Ratepayers in areas of high owner occupation, and, other things being equal, the level of support will be related proportionately to the density of owner occupation in the electoral wards.

Statistical testing shows this to be a reasonably accurate prediction. Thirteen wards were contested by a Ratepayer candidate at every election between 1975 and 1979 (inclusive). Using these cases as the core area of Ratepayer support, we tested the relationship by using the Spearman Rank Correlation Coefficient (which is a method for measuring the degree of correspondence between two sets of figures). The result (r_s = .434) is within the range indicating that the relationship is sufficiently strong for it not to be a chance occurrence. Local factors, such as strong or weak candidates, or the strength of the 'resentment' vote, or changes in the tenure pattern after the 1971 census (the source of the owner occupier base), may weaken the relationship. Despite these reservations the correlation gives an indication of a definite correspondence between the degree of Ratepayer support and owner occupation.

The spatial distribution of the two main tenure categories is an important part of the equation because Barnsley contains a relatively high level of local intermixing of owner occupied and council rented housing (Clutton, 1974). In addition, the social class composition across the District is predominantly manual worker. The index of skilled manual workers is particularly high, higher on average than the other areas of South Yorkshire (Coates, 1974), reaching peak values of 60–70 per cent of the heads of households in the outlying wards of the district – areas where the Ratepayer challenge has been particularly strong. The combination of an owner occupier/skilled manual worker social base is fertile ground for ratepayer politics. This proposition finds an echo in the analysis of the 1979 general election, which suggested that under certain circumstances skilled manual workers break more easily with established voting patterns than manual workers as a whole (Crewe, 1979). Dunleavy's thesis that consumption interests exert a stronger influence on voting alignments than occupational class is important in this context because voting for a Ratepayer candidate is an overtly consumption-weighted vote, both in the context of the ratepayer ideology and the specific appeal of their electoral programme. Although it is an axiom of political science that voting behaviour in local elections predominantly reflects national politics (see Chapter 1) there is strong evidence in this analysis that support for Ratepayer candidates cross-cuts national party alignments and therefore suggests the presence of a locally focused consumption factor in local politics. The pattern of support given to Ratepayer candidates in the 1979 local elections in Barnsley provides the clearest evidence of the existence of this pervasive factor.

The 1979 local election

Interest in the 1979 local election was heightened in Barnsley not only because of the simultaneous general election, but also because it was an 'all-out' election for the District Council due to some boundary revisions. The electors had four votes to cast: one to support their parliamentary candidate and up to three to cast for their local government members, although they were not bound to use all three of these votes. On the basis of an expected high poll, the Labour Party was predicting a clean sweep of the local seats on a par with the result at the previous all-out election in 1973. In fact the Ratepayers' Association, fielding thirty-nine candidates, increased its representation to eighteen members and took 30 per cent of the votes cast, which was better than its 1975–8 average. The remarkable feature of this election was the very high rate of cross-party voting which, in some wards, amounted to a collapse of party partisanship as an explanation of the result. In the outlying Cudworth ward, for example, in a straight fight between three Labour and three Ratepayer candidates, the voters chose, at the head of the poll, one of the Labour candidates, with two Ratepayers taking the remaining two seats followed in the list by the other two Labour candidates, and the remaining Ratepayer last. In Penistone East the voters returned one Ratepayer, one Conservative and one Labour candidate, with startling vote dispersions of nearly 1500 separating the best and worst Labour candidates and over 1000 votes the best and worst Conservatives. With a majority of over 18,000 for Roy Mason in the constituency election, a large number of people must have voted Labour in the general election and some combination of cross-party vote, which included a Ratepayer, in the local elections. What accounts for this unusual pattern of voting behaviour?

There is a strong indication that voters were discriminating in favour of selected personalities, particularly sitting councillors, the total picture suggesting a much higher level of knowledge about local politicians than is often suggested. For example, there was little evidence of the influence on the result of the alphabetic order of candidates on the ballot paper (within party slates) which Hampton (1968) detected in an all-out election in Sheffield. The same statistical test used by Hampton produced a very marginal tendency towards alphabetic preference, but certainly nothing like the very strong pattern found in the Sheffield multi-vote election. The voters in Barnsley were making conscious and not accidental choices as a result of being confronted by an unusually long ballot paper.

The primary factor that accounts for the extraordinary degree of cross-party voting (compared to the previous all-out election in 1973) was the pattern of support given to the Ratepayer candidates. The key feature of this support was that it cross-cut national party alignments, on the same day as a general election, with Ratepayers drawing votes from both Labour and Conservative supporters in national politics. The reasons for this relate to the substantive elements in the ideologies and political programme of ratepayer politics, iden-tified earlier in the chapter. In the context of an unusual combination of factors in the local election, a high turnout due to the national elections, a slate of Ratepayer candidates in most wards, and the all-out contest, the political expression of the ideologies around the rates issue were heightened. For the first time voters had a choice of expressing a partial anti-Labour vote by spreading their choices across the parties. This provided an opportunity for a locally focused expression of the key ratepayer ideology to surface. The specific programme offered by the Ratepayers' Association generated support from owner occupiers that was so directly geared to this ideology that it attracted, in its local form, a large number of people who nevertheless voted Labour at the national election.

Rates are a local form of taxation to provide local services, and this characteristic of the rates issue cuts across the nationally structured component of the ratepayer ideology (the differential perception of owner occupiers as unsubsidised ratepayers and council tenants as subsidised non-ratepayers). Because of the element of localism involved in the ratepayer ideology it is bound to be a potent force in local elections if circumstances allow it to emerge. In the 1979 elections in Barnsley conditions were ideal. These included some of the enduring consequences of local government reorganisation – a series of high rate increases, a political vacuum left by the collapse of the anti-Labour groups in the context of a metropolitan scale of politics, and a 'resentment' vote, especially in outlying wards of the new District, against the overbearing influence of the political and administrative machine of the old Barnsley Borough Council.

Within the Ratepayer manifesto many elements of the public/private sector ideologies in local politics are explicit: the attacks on the Direct Works Department and the Planning Department as 'extravagances', the idea of tendering in the private market for the provision of urban public services, and support for the sale of council houses. Closely related to this is the anti-party politics stance of the Ratepayer programme, which is an implicitly anti-Labour position, focusing on Labour's advocacy of public sector services and generally as the party of 'welfare'. This is a particularly pronounced feature of the political situation in solidly Labour-supporting areas such as Barnsley and is the key explanation for the existence of ratepayer movements in South Wales and the North of England in the post-1974 context. It is not just the absence of a history of Conservative opposition that conditions the emergence of ratepayer organisations, but also the dominance of Labour.

Whether the ratepayers' organisation is capable of sustaining its support is questionable. Descriptions of other post-1974 ratepayer movements suggest an inevitable pattern of internal faction fighting and personality clashes leading to rapid collapse. The Barnsley organisation is a case in point.

The ratepayer organisation

Barnsley and District Ratepayers' Association consists of a loose federation of groups based on the electoral wards. They refute the notion that they are a political party and claim to draw support from people of all party political persuasions; their electoral performance indicates that this is the case. They argue, as we have seen, that it is necessary to enter the electoral arena in order to wrest control of local spending decisions from the party-dominated system. The vast majority of their effort is concerned with contesting the local elections and servicing their elected representatives. Individual membership is made by payment of a small fee, but these ordinary members – claimed to be 15,000 strong in the initial phase – play an insignificant role in the organisation. The small group of activists at the centre of the group are comprised mainly of the Ratepayer group of councillors. By occupation these people are either middle-tier managers, private sector professionals or self-employed small businessmen. It is a middle-class leadership with a strong entrepreneurial ethos and drawn predominantly from private sector occupations. Given the ideological stance of the ratepayer movement, it is not surprising to find such a heavy concentration of core activists drawn from this range of backgrounds. In the early period a number of trade union activists dabbled with ratepayer politics as a route of entry into local affairs denied to them for various reasons by the Labour Party. An NUM official, for example, was elected on a Ratepayer ticket in a by-election in 1977, but five months later he applied for Labour Party membership and joined the Labour group of councillors. He successfully defended the seat for Labour the following May. The loose federation of Ratepayer branches has not held disenchanted Labourites for very long.

In the late 1970s tensions between the branches and the central group emerged around the question of who makes policy, but as the main opposition group in the local council the leadership was able to enforce a rudimentary discipline. In November 1980 the announcement of a supplementary rate demand resulted in 400 new applications for membership. But in the run-up to the 1982 elections a number of defections took place from the front rank of Ratepayer activists when the chairman of the group of councillors and a number of his supporters joined the new Social Democratic Party. The Ratepayers were, nevertheless, able to mount a creditable campaign, and in the wards they contested did better on average than the SDP, with Labour reaping the benefit of a split anti-Labout vote. This is likely to be a pattern for the future. The social base on which the Ratepayers built their success in the 1974–81 period will continue to be alive to the appeal of their programme, but mounting an annual election campaign without much intervening activity makes a viable organisation difficult to sustain. The objective conditions and the subjective capability are not necessarily contingent.

Previous descriptions of ratepayer organisations have treated the periodic emergency of ratepayer movements as ephemeral to mainstream local politics. They are discussed either as examples of 'middle-class' politics or in terms of the conditions that might give rise to a ratepayers' association. By taking them as a form of urban social movement it is possible to make a more specific assessment of their place in the local political system. In particular ratepayer movements are indicators of the existence of a number of core ideologies within local politics – the ratepayer ideology and the public/private sector dichotomy – and, closely related to these, the existence of a key sectoral division built around the primary housing tenures. Two historical facets in this process of ideological structuring which directly fed into the conditions that underlie ratepayer politics have been identified: first, the historical precedence of private property as a source of citizenship confronted by the rise of Labour in municipal government; and second, the closely related theme of the expansion of owner occupancy and council tenancy in the pre-1945 decades. In the post-1945 era, Dunleavy shows that these sectoral divisions established the basis for district consumption-based conflicts which cut across the social class system.

Sectoral politics and the related ideologies provide the basic elements of the ratepayer social base and political programme. The Ratepayers' Association in Barnsley is probably the best example nationally of the combination of events and underlying conditions appropriate to a relatively sustained political intervention based on the politics of the rates issue. First, the degree of intermixing of the two main tenure categories in the context of a predominantly skilled manual worker population provided a fertile social base. Second, the pre-eminence of the Labour Party in local politics provided a political history and system highly vulnerable to the anti-party, anti-public service critique that are central tenets of the ratepayer programme. The absence of a Conservative opposition party and the creation of a Metropolitian District in the 1973 reorganisation from a large number of administrative/political fragments, combined to create a political vacuum that the Ratepayers' Association was able to fill.

This type of political movement should be treated as more than an epiphenomenal feature of localised concern if only because they point to, and in the case of ratepayer movements, symbolise, the existence of the deep-level ideological structuring of local political systems. Ratepayer movements are significant because they draw on consumption interests that not only cut across traditional party political alignments but also suggest that the locally focused consumption stakes, built on the rates issue, are sufficiently strong to break even the dominant pattern of the nationalisation of local elections.

Ratepayers' associations represent a conservative force in local politics and show that issues within the social consumption arena are contested by organisations which span the political spectrum. More specifically they are drawn from a social base representing the private sector in the housing market which is linked through their political programme to a critique of whole areas of urban public service provision. The same ideological terrain and political consequences can be sketched out from a discussion of a 'radical' form of urban social movement, the squatters' movement.

The squatters' movement

Unlike the sparse literature on ratepayer politics, the squatters' movement has been extensively documented and is the subject of two authoritative bibliographies (Self-Help Housing Resource Library, 1980; Paris and Poppleston, 1978). There are innumerable short case studies, and readers are referred to the collection of articles in *Squatting: The Real Story* (Wates and Wolmar, 1980) for some of the most vivid accounts. Squatting is a form of urban protest which focuses on and confronts a crucial political and ideological issue; of private property rights versus housing for need. Available sources indicate that, at least in London, the squatting movement, but by no means all squatting, was concentrated in empty public sector accommodation. The basic theme is to question how it was that the issue of private property 'rights' was transformed into a generalised critique of the public sector (Cant, 1976; Dunleavy, 1980; Wates and Wolmar, 1980). If this is the case it provides an important insight into the way in which even supposedly radical urban social movements are manipulated by the ideological and institutional support mechanisms of the dominant private sector. In this process the evidence indicates once again the crucial significance of key local system ideologies working through representative local democracy and the public/private sectoral divide. The following account describes some of the main features of this very diverse and eclectic social movement, discusses the significance of the sectoral split in the squatting movement and why it arose, and, finally, sums up on the structuring of the movement under the influence of key ideologies.

Squatting as a social movement

Although large numbers of people have for centuries lived in unconventional surroundings either by choice or from force of necessity, there have been several periods in the era of national housing policies when distinct squatting movements have emerged. These social movements, rather than the innumerable isolated, individual squats, have made a distinct impact and won a range of concessions from the housing authorities. To some extent they have been welcomed by local authorities as a means of relieving pressure on scarce housing resources, but the overwhelming response, orchestrated by sustained and largely unscrupulous media attention, has been one of hostility and suspicion.

Two major squatting movements developed nationally in the aftermath of the two world wars. Demobilised servicemen and their families formed the nucleus of these movements, which enjoyed widespread public support. In 1945 squatters occupied the large lodging houses in the south coast resorts of Brighton and Hastings. Within a matter of weeks the 'Secret Committee of Ex-Servicemen', known as the Vigilantes, had installed over 1,000 people into accommodation, usually by clandestine operations during the night. In 1946 a second wave of squatting activity developed around the occupation of empty army camps; by the autumn some 45,000 people were squatting in 1,000 ex-service camps (Friend, 1980). But once the movement spread to fashionable parts of London's West End, the tide of media comment and government quiescence turned against the movement. Bevan spuriously denounced the squatters in ex-service camps for diverting building materials from the public housing programme. He hoped that this tactic would distract attention from the bureaucratic delays in the government's own house-building programme.

Partly because of the failure to integrate the squatters' organisations into the wider working-class movement, and partly through the impact of adverse press comment, the squatters' movement quickly fragmented, leading to large-scale evictions and the continuation of a squalid and unserviced Nissan hut existence for thousands of families. Many of the London squatters were eventually rehoused by the local authorities, and the whole 1945–6 squatting episode was put down to the exceptional post-war circumstances, while the long-term and underlying issue of homelessness and housing need were absorbed into government-subsidised public and private sector house building programmes. It was assumed that if a large enough quantity of houses were built, homelessness would disappear. Apart from the enduring problems of the immediate post-war years there is no record of a squatting activity, except by isolated handfuls of individuals, in the 1950s and most of the 1960s; there was certainly no squatters' movement.

Despite the massive building programme it was apparent by the mid-1960s that homelessness had not only not disappeared but was increasing rapidly. This was largely a consequence of the national urban renewal programme underpinned by corporate involvement in mass construction housing provision, and property speculation. The redevelopment process caused 'planning blight', typically creating valueless streets of sparsely populated accommodation. Furthermore, due to the adverse investment value of private renting and the unsubsidised state of this sector, many landlord-owners chose to keep their property empty. In the early 1970s the London Boroughs Association claimed that over 40,000 privately owned houses in London had been empty for over a year (Watkinson and Reed, 1976). Awareness of the extent of homelessness in London was heightened by the famous television programme, 'Cathy Come Home', screened for the first time in 1966.

At the same time activists from within CND and the Vietnam Solidarity Campaign were taking more interest in urban politics (Platt, 1980). This is the reverse of the trend noted by Ceccarelli in the recent period, and further demonstrates the important area of osmosis between urban movements and wider political movements. Some of these people had already been involved in the bitterly fought dispute at the King Hill Hostel in West Malling, Kent in 1965–6. Kent County Council had been forced to change its rules, excluding fathers of homeless families from the hostels, by the direct action of husbands who moved in and refused to leave. Among the people involved in this campaign was Ron Bailey. He and a small group of activists, convinced that direct action could achieve rapid results, formed the London Squatters Campaign (LSC) following the third screening of 'Cathy Come Home' in November 1968 (Bailey, 1973). The aim of the group was described as 'the rehousing of families from hostels or slums by means of squatting'. But the campaign clearly had the wider intention of forcing central and local government to adopt new approaches to helping families in housing need. The London Squatters Campaign marked the birth of a new and distinct housing movement which became a model for hundreds of squatters' groups. After a series of token squats in luxury apartment blocks, LSC activists organised systematic squatting in empty houses in a redevelopment area in the London Borough of Redbridge. The council reacted with unsuccessful attempts to serve possession orders and later sanctioned the use of private bailiffs to evict the families. But media coverage of the evictions, also unsuccessful, compelled Redbridge Council to negotiate with the squatters. In its struggle against the local authority, LSC used a variety of tactics that were to become commonplace community action methods – organising publicity events, demonstrations in council meetings, picketing the homes of authority officers. Far from simply fixing up squats they had become a fully fledged urban social movement.

As part of its success in staving off the bailiffs, the Redbridge campaign also established an important legal precedent, that landlords should seek eviction through the use of court orders only. But the crucial feature of LSC action was to focus attention on the bureaucratic nature of local authority housing provision. At its outset the squatters' movement of the 1970s began to take on a very definite sectoral bias, broadly critical of and actively targeted against the public sector. The core issue of principle involved in squatting, the critique of private property rights, rapidly became lost in a maze of negotiations and campaigns against local councils. As Platt observes, 'Squatting in Redbridge was not so much a challenge to private property rights as it was to incompetent councils' (Platt, 1980).

The character of the early private squats was very different from those in the public sector, and these differences had the effect of reinforcing the rapidly developing cleavage between the sectors. They also had some generally harmful long-term repercussions on the whole squatting movement. Squats in privately owned accommodation tended to gravitate towards the ideological extremes of the anti-private property terrain. On the one hand, much private sector squatting was totally non-political; people squatted out of sheer necessity, having failed to obtain access to suitable or sufficiently cheap housing by other means. (The limited evidence suggests that this is the dominant motivation for all squatters. Platt's survey found that less than 10 per cent of his sample of squatters in Haringey had done so either 'as a protest' or 'to get involved in some sort of social or political action' (Platt, 1980).) The contrary tendency in the private sector was for squats to be laid for overtly political reasons. The hippy squats in Central London in the late 1960s, for example, had strong anarchist and libertarian tendencies. The fact that they often chose to squat in prestigious privately owned buildings was treated as a much higher level of threat by the authorities, and the squats were frequently broken up by police intervention within days of the occupation. These squats also became the subjects of virulent media misrepresentation and manipulation. The short squat in 144 Piccadilly was greeted with a barrage of fantastic press invention, and despite stories of hippies and Hell's Angels armed to the teeth, the eviction was almost entirely peaceful. But the Piccadilly squat and other similar situations had the double effect of irrevocably discrediting the popular image of the squatting movement, and of diverting public attention from the real issue of the plight facing thousands of single, young homeless people.

The sectoral division in the squatting movement was clearcut by the end of the 1960s. A majority of squatting appeared to be taking place in the public sector, and much of it was organised through community action groups. Initially, at least, public opinion was supportive. In the private sector the squats were either not organised or were precociously libertarian and were subject to hostile media reaction and swift police intervention.

In the public sector squats, the late 1960s saw the development of another important and controversial divide. In July 1969 the government issued a circular urging local authorities to make use of short-life property by a system of licensing their use to tenants. Lewisham council was already negotiating with South East London Squatters for the licensed use of some of their stock of empty houses in redevelopment areas. Aware that these properties were likely to be squatted anyway, and wishing to avoid a repetition of the violent events in Redbridge, Lewisham conceded the principle of licensing. This gave the squatters a legal right to be in the property but on condition that they vacated it as soon as the licence was revoked. Public sector squatting has had two quite distinct wings, those that are licensed and those that are unlicensed. The implications of this will be discussed in the next section. It is sufficient here to say that demand for accommodation far outweighed the amount of property the local authorities had or were prepared to tie up in licensing agreements. Unlicensed squatting continued to mushroom into the peak period in 1975-6 when one estimate puts the figure of squats (licensed and unlicensed) in Britain in excess of 50,000 (Wates and Wolmar, 1980). Waugh's analysis of the figures concluded that in 1976 there were between 10,000 and 50,000 squats in the country (Waugh, 1976).

As the numerical explosion of squatting reached its peak, so the barrage of hostile media comment intensified to a crescendo. The relatively fragmented squatters' movement was ill-equipped to counter-attack. Platt argues that this situation led to an important change in the movement. 'Many squatters' reaction to the onslaught was to play down the fact that they were squatting. To appease neighbours, some even pretended they were not squatters and were paying rent. More positively, an increasing number of squatters began to organise in a variety of ways to cope with the threat' (Platt, 1980, p. 64.) This new phase took a variety of forms, but characteristically involved the formation of street and neighbourhood level squatting groups. These were functional groups that organised news sheets, co-operative repair work, bargaining with owners and the public authorities, and finding alternative premises in the event of eviction. The most successful of these groups, such as the Elgin Road squat (Corbyn, 1980), had already sunk roots in the areas, but these were a minority and many badly organised squats were terminated by eviction at this time. A number of attempts were made to organise city-wide federations to co-ordinate defensive strategies, but none were more than partially success-ful and often relied heavily on a few activists. Some of the best organised squatting activity eventually led to the establishment of housing co-ops or to the absorption of the squatted properties into Housing Associations, recognised and funded by the Housing Corporation. Several groups took advantage of the encouragement given to these forms of quasi-public sector housing organisations by the 1974 Housing Act (Wood, 1980). But this process involved continuous organisation over a period of years, and professional negotiating abilities which the generally shifting and low-skill squatter community did not possess. By 1978 there were only eight listed housing co-ops that had emerged out of squatting organisations (information from the Co-operative Housing Agency in 1978).

By the end of the 1970s, squatting as an organised movement had virtually collapsed. Some groups were tolerated so long as the housing was not immediately needed by the authorities. But after years of struggle and harassment, the movement disin-tegrated. Thousands of individuals continue to resort to squat-ting as a last desperate attempt to secure some form of accommodation, but the squatting movement is anathema to the 'new Right' political environment of the 1980s.

The sectoral division of the squatting movement

Numerical measurement of the extent of squatting is inherently problematic, and there are no reliable sources that have compared the scale of squatting activity in public and privately owned properties. It is assumed by most observers that there is a concentration of squats in the public housing sector. Certainly most of the organised squatting movements have focused on empty public property, and the bulk of press coverage and general debate would seem to support the view that public sector housing has been the main target. In addition, the evidence on private squatting suggests that there has not been anywhere near the number of organised movements compared to the public sector. Why should this be the case? Why on the one hand was the squatting movement in the 1970s under-represented in private void property, and why, on the other hand, did the organisational forms taken by private sector squatters take on a largely non-political character? There are very strong arguments, given that squatting as an activity implies a critical view of the concept of private property rights, for thinking that it would be precisely in the private sector that a concentration of squats might be predicted. The ideological battle would appear to be most poignant around privately owned property.

Moreover, as Cant (1976) and Wates and Wolmar (1980) show, there are two additional practical factors that underpin the argument of principle. First, the reasons why public and private sector property is left unoccupied differ, and second, the numbers of empty properties and length of time they are left vacant also varies across the sectors.

Most vacant dwellings in the public sector arise from planned policy decisions which often become caught up in lengthy management and plan implementation delays. This is par-ticularly the case where a local authority has initiated a rolling programme of renovation or of clearance. In either case unforeseen problems invariably create bottlenecks. These may be caused by financial restrictions, by drawn-out compulsory purchase procedures, problems of mobilising in sequence a variety of specialist private contractors to undertake repair or demolition work, and so on. Most local authorities in addition routinely allow a small proportion of their stock to be empty due to the complex allocation procedures, and most large authorities have 'difficult-to-let' estates. Despite the bureaucratic delay often involved in these processes, the reasons for houses being empty are within the ambit of publicly defined policy. So far as the private sector is concerned, however, this is not the case. The vast majority of private void property is created for speculative financial gain for the owners. Large-scale property developers are able to blight streets and even whole neighbourhoods by leaving properties empty prior to seeking planning permission for redevelopment. Or owners simply leave houses vacant in order to reap the benefit of the investment value of the property. At least since the mid-1960s, and probably earlier, house prices have inflated faster than the general index of price increases.

The second factor that might have implied a concentration of squatting activity in privately owned housing is the relative scale and rate of increase of void properties in the private compared to the public sector. Although conditions vary from area to area, and the statistics reflect different survey procedures, or lack of them, in different local authorities, the evidence in London indicates anything from a two-to-one to a five-to-one ratio of private to public voids (Cant, 1976; Wates and Wolmar, 1980). The data also convincingly show that the average length of time private void dwellings are kept empty is much longer than in the public sector. These factors again imply the prediction of at least a majority of squatting activity in the private sector if only because there is more of it and it is vacant for longer periods. But this has not in fact been the case. The explanation for this arises from the way in which squatting opportunities were perceived, the differential enforcement procedures between public and private squats by the courts and police, and an early experience of dealing with public housing authorities at the beginning of the new squatting movement in the late 1960s. Following the adverse publicity surrounding the eviction of squatters in Redbridge, local authorities were more cautious in their use of private bailiffs. Illegal and clandestine evictions were more likely in private sector squats. Despite the growing quantity of empty private sector property the owners and landlords became adept at disguising empty property by maintaining minimum furnishings; the visibility of such property was generally lower than in the public sector, where empty properties tended to cluster in areas subject to clearance or rehabilitation plans. As Cant argues in his study of the question of public and private sector squatting.

> Local government is in the public eye, hence the potential squatter can find out more easily about public sector voids. Squatters in public sector property could also claim some spurious justification for their acts on the grounds that the state is obliged to provide housing for those in need. (Cant, 1976, p. 66)

The perceived role of local authorities as providers of housing for need strongly supported the emphasis on public sector squatting. As a visible public body, local housing authorities were easier to bargain with, and at an early stage revealed their vulnerability to organised pressure. Because of the different functions of the public and private sectors, the general field of the debate rapidly came to focus on the bureaucratic inefficiencies of local planners and housing department officials in the phasing of plan implementation and the management of the allocation process. These 'problems' became a focal point because they were amenable to negotiation in a way that an overt challenge to private owners to choose to keep their property empty if they so wished was not.

The licensing issue

Although it is justified to make a distinction between 'hard' (private sector) and 'soft' (public sector) squats (Dunleavy, 1980, p. 159), it would be misleading to characterise public sector squatting as in any way acceptable to the local state. Public landlords operate in the context of the dominant ethos of ownership, and used the imagery and language of the private sector to oppose squatters in 'their' housing. Most local authorities totally opposed squatters, fearing that any display of compromise would make them a target area for squatting action. The tactics adopted against them typically included pronouncements about 'firm but fair' action, but in practice involved a continuous level of harassment and eviction, the systematic gutting of squattable dwellings, and cutting the supply of services. Local authorities that conceded licensing agreements and tacit recognition of some squatting activity were predominantly those authorities under greatest numerical pressure by virtue of their location and policy programmes. Elsewhere the public sector authorities, without the same force of judicial sanction and ideological weight to support them, used their own methods to deal with the 'problem'.

Licensing, however, was a very difficult issue for public sector squatters, and from the time that South East London Squatters closed the deal with Lewisham Council the squatting movement based in local authority properties effectively had two wings, licensed and unlicensed squats. The problem was what to do when the local authorities revoked the licences. At its peak in the mid-1970s, licensing agreements covered probably no more than 3000 squatters in sixteen London boroughs (Platt, 1980, p. 29). This represented not so much a concession to the squatting movement as a tactical ploy in circumstances where squatting was most numerically concentrated. Licensing had the distinct advantage of appearing to regularise an inherently irregular situation. It was fundamentally about creating a display of control and was intended to pacify criticisms by the media and local elite networks of local authorities that 'allowed' squatting. It gave councils a propaganda base from which to justify hardline action and evictions against 'illegitimate' (i.e. unlicensed) squatters. In addition, the fact that most licensed squats were occupied by families was acceptable because it eased the waiting lists of people for whom the housing authorities would otherwise probably have been responsible. Licensing is a classic example of the co-option of a critical social movement. By drawing some groups into bureaucratic administrative procedures, the local authorities further fragmented the movement and established a justification for harassing the majority of unlicensed squatters.

Ideologies and the squatting movement

Two of the major ideologies that structure the local political system (see Chapter 3), the ideology of representative local democracy and the ideologies around the public/private sectoral divide, played a crucial part in the development and characteristics of squatting as an urban movement in Britain in the 1970s.

The notion of a publicly accountable local authority was crucial to the early concentration of squatting activity in the public sector. It was argued either explicitly or implicitly by the squatters that because local councils have duties to provide housing on the basis of need, and because of their inability, largely through bureaucratic maladministration, to achieve this aim, squatting in empty public sector property is a justifiable response. The focus of this dispute was frequently the waiting-list system of allocating council houses, the squatters arguing that their action reduced pressure on it, by utilising properties that would not otherwise be occupied, while the councillors frequently criticised squatters for bucking the system (of democratically sanctioned procedures) or queue-jumping. There can be little doubt that the weight of argument decisively favours the squatters' argument, not only because squats have rarely taken place in accommodation that was eligible for allocation to the waiting list, but also because waiting lists are not routinely structured or used on the basis of merit. As Gray argues,

> In those authorities where demand greatly outweighs supply the waiting list appears a most ineffectual and subjective instrument of selecting households . . . the discretionary power of local authorities to rehouse special cases may result in a slight or non-existent turnover in the list (Gray, 1979).

Moreover, in a large number of local authorities in the 1970s single young people were not eligible to put their names on the lists, and as a high proportion of new squatters in the 1970s were drawn precisely from that stratum of society, the notion of queue-jumping was perverse. The key point here is the recognition of the way that the local democratic ideology on the one hand focused the activity of the squatting movement on public housing; at the same time, the same ideological source provides the major anti-squatting arguments and legitimised a broadly repressive policy approach.

There is also a crucial area of overlap with the public/private sector ideology. Here the dominant private sector – with more empty properties than the public sector and empty for longer periods – was able to deflect attention from the central issue of private property rights. Property and its ownership by private individuals is the core of the dominant economic and political system; there is nothing more fundamental. As Cant observes, 'the fundamental issue at stake in the squatting movement . . . was the right of landlords to keep their property empty for reasons of personal profit at a time of homelessness' (Cant, 1976, p. 67). This ground can literally not be conceded. The key issue was lost by default at an early stage. The mechanisms were judicial enforcement, police intervention and an orchestrated media campaign against 'political' squats. That section of the squatting movement which did attempt to confront the heartland of the property system was by definition libertarian (i.e. *anti*-private property) and outside the bounds of the political culture. Because they targeted some of the most conspicuous void properties they were swiftly dispatched, but in the process created a backlash against the whole squatting movement. Thereafter the sectoral balance shifted decisively away from the private sector and the squatting movement focused most of its activity into the public arena, where empty property was more visible, the squats easier to lay, and the owners publicly accountable and vulnerable to political campaigns.

Conclusion

The two types of urban social movement discussed in this chapter illustrate the ways in which the formation and characterisation of political protest in local politics is profoundly affected by the existence of a number of core ideologies. Although they stand in contrasting relations to the dominant private property market, both sets of organisations have been shaped by the mediating orthodoxies of representative local democracy and by the historical and contemporary impact of private versus public solutions to the provision of the urban-based consumption services. The ratepayer movements, recoiling from the long-term political control of Labour in some areas of the country, take a virulent anti-rates/anti-public sector stance. This is not only critical of public sector provision; it campaigns for a fundamental shift of resources away from publicly subsidised service provision and towards free-market and competitive purchase. They argue that the notion of democratic accountability in local government has been corrupted by party politics and seek a populist return of power to 'the people'. It has been argued here that the owner occupier/ council tenant tenure dichotomy was the basis of their political support, drawing from a social base rooted in home ownership and structured by a pervasive ratepayer ideology.

The squatting movement developed in the late 1960s in response to the growth of homelessness and voids in the housing stock. This movement rapidly split on a sectoral basis, with the public sector attracting a disporportionate degree of squatting activity compared to the number and duration of empty properties in the two sectors. The reasons for this were ascribed to the differential treatment, on the one hand by the judicial and police authorities, and on the other hand by the media, of the squatters in the private and public sectors. Some politically libertarian private sector squats, challenging the fundamental 'rights' of private property ownership, were quickly broken up. The public sector, however, was seen to be more open to criticism as the housing stock is controlled by publicly accountable bodies. The empty properties often clustered on an areal basis, enabling the formation of local squatting groups, some of which campaigned for the better use of void public sector housing. Private sector squatting campaigns were rapidly curbed, leaving only vulnerable, non-political and individualised squats.

The ratepayers' and squatters' movements were seen as being harnessed to a number of key ideologies that structure the local political system: the orthodoxy of representative local democracy and the public/private sectoral dichotomy in local service provision. The ideology of accountability – asserting a false relationship between policy outputs and citizen involvement mediated by the ballot box – was the basis of the ratepayers' campaign against the long-term, oligarchic, party political control of local government; and in the squatters' movement it was the justification for the critique of the public housing authorities, simply because they are accountable bodies. The public/private sector ideology, asserting the dominance of private market solutions over subsidised public management of the urban services, formed the basis of a ratepayer programme keyed directly into an ideologically structured social base. This same powerful and highly potent ideology was seen in the case of the squatters' movement to deflect a potentially damaging assault on the private sector into the exactly parallel criticism made by the ratepayers of public planning and housing policy and administration.

Two types of urban social movement representing diametrically opposed social bases within the domestic property system – owners and the propertyless – and with highly contrasting political perspectives, illustrate how key ideologies operate to structure the apparently intangible relationships between the mass of ordinary people and the dominant economic and political order.

Chapter 6

Comparative Urban Social Movements

Chapters 1 and 2 were concerned with criticisms of Castells's recent model of urban social change. Particular attention was paid to a range of methodological problems with his text *The City and the Grassroots*, which cast doubt on whether he could justifiably claim either to have established definitive criteria for the characterisation and analysis of urban social movements, or to have defined the contents of an all-embracing cross-cultural theory of urban social change.

Castells's use of the Madrid Citizens' Movement as an archetypal model of an urban social movement was questioned because of a validation problem with his evidence: whether, in the terms of his model, the Madrid movement offered sufficient grounds to sustain his claims, and whether the exceptional political and historical context in which the movement developed could be a valid basis for a generalised, comparative theory. It is to the latter issue that this chapter is specifically addressed. What parallels can usefully be drawn between the great diversity of urban movements that exist across the globe? Does the state of our knowledge allow for purposive generalised model-building? If it does, what are the key interactive elements that link cross-national and cross-cultural experiences of urban protest and urban social change? How can we account in model-building for the fundamental economic and ideological divides that structure world politics – between development and underdevelopment, between corporate state capitalism and bureaucratically deformed socialist states? There is a danger in premature modelling because it may obscure more than it reveals. This danger is implicit in Castells's cross-cultural theory of urban social change. A thematic focus would be a more fruitful line of advance rather than an emphasis on building structurally conditioned definitions and models.

This chapter begins with an example of the type of problem that has arisen as a result of Castells's position, involving the assessment of the level of urban-based political action across the globe in the current period. This leads to a consideration of the basis on which the comparative analysis or urban social movements should be made. The approach adopted involves examining evidence from groups of related countries or individual nations on their experience of urban political activity in the last decade. From this follows a discussion of the usefulness or otherwise of comparative models. Castells's thesis is briefly recalled and an alternative set of propositions subsequently put forward by Pickvance is discussed, with an evaluation of these models against the case studies. These case studies have been selected from a range of contrasting economic and political systems – Southern Europe, the United States of America, the People's Republic of Poland and Latin America – to establish which factors can most usefully be employed in the cross-cultural analysis of urban movements.

Models of change – the growth or decline of urban social movements?

An important theme in some of the recent comparative discussion of urban politics, and from which competing theoretical models have evolved, concerns the interpretation of the scale and intensity of movement-based activity in the latter part of the 1970s. Castells, for example, points to an 'uneven development of urban movements, but of expansion to a broader geographical and cultural area' (1983, p. 327). Thus while the Italian experience of urban protest seemed to wane in the mid-1970s, so the Spanish neighbourhood movement was at its peak; this in turn, following its eclipse after 1979, was replaced by the squatters' movements in Holland and Germany. In his bibliography, Castells lists hundreds of books, articles and studies describing urban protest organisations and concludes,

> In spite of the absence of reliable, systematic information on the development of urban movements in different countries throughout history, our own knowledge as well as the amount of existing information suggest a clear, comparative upward trend. (Castells, 1983, p. 328)

Although admitting uneven development, the notion of a continuous rise in urban political activity based on quantitative evidence must be highly questionable. Castells's interpretation inevitably flows from the gradually evolving emphasis he comes to place on the 'urban' or the 'city' as the source of social change (see Chapter 1), so that once again he is caught in a methodological tautology – an upswing is a necessary part of his theoretical proposition. But there is important evidence from other sources that, far from there being a sustained growth of urban movements, the last decade has in fact been a period of slow-down or even elimination. Pickvance goes so far as to suggest that

> The study of urban movements has a problem: urban movements have ceased to exist . . . To be more accurate urban movements have undergone a dramatic decline in those societies – especially in Western Europe – where they were most active. (Pickvance, 1983, p. 1)

The notion of a lull in urban movement activity has also been analysed on a comparative basis by Ceccarelli, who argues that

> Large-scale urban social movements have faded out as rapidly as they originated and no longer play the role that they did in the political process of the past decade. (Ceccarelli, 1982, p. 261).

Ceccarelli's observation about the changed role of urban movements is significant because it leads him to consider not only the basis on which the movements have declined, but to make an assessment of the place of urban politics in political systems and the criteria on which a comparative evaluation might be made. Other commentators have also raised the question of the changed nature of urban protest in the late 1970s and 1980s in the context of discussions about single countries (Evers, 1981; Marcelloni, 1979). This discussion mostly concerns the situation in Europe and, despite reference to some sporadic outbursts of violent or militant protest, the main picture is one of dramatically reduced scale and intensity of urban-based protest movements. Ceccarelli makes a more specific claim for this pattern of events when he argues, 'European countries which experienced the highest political mobilization in the 1960s and 1970s are at present the ones where urban movements appear to be almost nonexistent' (Ceccarelli, 1982, p. 265). He mentions in particular Italy, France and Spain. We will focus on those countries in the next section because it is apparent that in the European context they have witnessed some of the most intense urban movement activity but entered a period of lull in the mid-1970s, although not simultaneously. What happened and what are the apparent similarities and differences in their experience?

Italy, France and Spain

The countries of Southern Europe share a common heritage in two key dimensions (Sharpe, 1979). First, their local and regional systems of government and administration have been strongly influenced by the Napoleonic model of the state. Second, they have all been the subject of rapid post-war industrialisation and very high levels of economic growth. This has been accompanied by high population movements generally involving a rural to urban migration pattern. But it is also the case that within these basic frameworks there have been important variations. For example, Spain and France share territorial/administrative divisions laid down in the early part of the nineteenth century – the fifty Spanish provinces and 8000 municipalities corresponded to French departments and communes, and in each country central government was responsible for appointing the civil governor of each area, who in turn appointed the municipal mayors. In both cases these officials sat at the head of the representative institutions and were empowered to overrule local decisions that were contrary to central state interests. But, unlike the French *préfet*, the Civil Governor in Spain was not a professional civil servant but a political appointee (Clegg, 1983). His function, in practice, involved overseeing social control and acting as a focal figure in the system of corrupt patronage known as the *caciquisimo*, designed largely to ensure alternation of power between the two monarchist parties (Carr, 1983, ch. 9). Central control has been deeply embedded in Spanish history, but so equally has reaction against its excesses and autocratic rule. As Clegg observes, 'the local level in Spanish politics was also the scene of repeated efforts to revolt against the central state and to establish a democratic regime' (Clegg, 1983, p. 5). A highly potent decentralist theme runs for 150 years through Spanish politics and surfaced, as we saw in Chapter 1, as a major strand in the opposition to the Franquist regime. While a strong centralist element is also present in France, this largely derives from the dominant influence of Paris as the geographical, demographic and historic core of the French nation and is counterbalanced by a more genuinely accountable and functional system of local government. The political and administrative traditions at regional and local level are key factors shaping the pattern and character of urban social movements and are, of course, overlaid by the historic condition of central-local relations.

The British case study material in Chapters 4 and 5 illustrates the structuring influence on urban political movements of the highly distinctive traditions of political control and administration in local government. Even a comparison between two nations – France and Spain – with a common heritage derived from the Napoleonic era and with a continuity of territorial divisions, indicates very significant variations in the experience and practice of local politics.

The second major factor structuring the recent histories of the Southern European states is the common experience of rapid post-war industrialisation and rapid economic growth. But again, the extent of this development, its timing and consequences have shown some crucial variations, particularly in relation to the process of urbanisation that accompanied industrial expansion. Of the three societies the earliest and most rapid post-war experience of industrialisation occurred in Italy. And it is in Italy where the most militant and large-scale urban protest occurred, and where it has most rapidly dissipated.

The process of conversion to an industrial society involving a large-scale rural exodus from Southern Italy was largely accomplished by the end of the 1950s. But, as Marcelloni argues, the so-called 'Italian miracle' was based on an unfettered exploitation of the workforce (Marcelloni, 1979). This took the form not only of low wages but of appalling lack of investment in the basic services, with the growth of squalid shanty towns especially in the formerly non-industrial cities where the basic infrastructure to cope with large-scale immigration was absent. In the 1950s some protest over the dreadful lack of public services and housing, and opposition to speculative private building, was apparent, particularly in Rome. However, it was not until the late 1960s that large-scale urban protest movements developed. These were set against the context of a radicalised working-class movement. The entry of the Italian Socialist Party (PSI) into a series of Centre-Left governments did not appease the growing strength of the radical working class, many of whom regarded the PSI involvement in government as a strategy of containment. Large-scale mass action shook the fabric of the society. The agenda of Italian politics had swung decisively away from the rigid and repressive regimes of the 1950s and 1960s towards the recognition that reform was needed to quell social unrest and industrial instability, now orchestrated by a powerful Communist Party (PCI) machine. At the same time, the Italian economy was beginning a new phase of capital-intensive investment.

The earlier period of rapid urbanisation had created squalid living conditions for many of the immigrant workers, particularly in Rome and Naples. This was the basis for differing patterns of urban protest between the southern and the northern cities in the 1960s and early 1970s. In the former, activity was very intensive. It was based on the marginalised shanty town dwellers who, in the desperate search for improved accommodation, squatted in empty public and private houses. As in London, there was a differential pattern of law enforcement between the sectors, with the private owners obtaining immediate police intervention. Resistance to evictions and the general organisation of urban movements in the south were led by activists from the left-wing parties. In the north in this period most of the activism still focused on factory-based disputes. Urban struggles were not regarded as important, and developed on an unco-ordinated and individual basis. This began to change, however, and gradually the whole country was engulfed in urban protest activity. Marcelloni argues that this change was caused by the control the communists had taken of the northern factories, which had the effect of driving out non-PCI militants into the urban arena. At the same time industrial workers in the northern cities were becoming more sensitive to non-workplace issues as the basic struggles for unions and wages were won (Marcelloni, 1979, p. 256).

This new situation of more intense and widespread urban political activity was met, however, with changes of strategy within the two major parties of the Left (PCI and PSI) that absorbed and contained the urban struggles. The effect was to begin a process of decline in the urban-orientated movements. There were two components involved. First, the parties, aware of the significance of the urban movements, adjusted their political programmes to take into account the issues being raised by the groups, and not only the issues as such but also the political methods – leading to more democratic and accountable decision-making processes. Second, the PCI in particular scored a succession of spectacular election victories in local government and was able, as Ceccarelli suggests, 'to answer, at least at the local level, some of the demands that urban movements had made in the most conflict-laden years' (Ceccarelli, 1982, p. 269). The effect of this new situation was the gradual withering away of urban movements in the latter 1970s. The grip of the Left parties on local government, and what was seen by some militant activists as the co-option of the Italian working-class movement into a reformist trap, led to a political polarisation. On the one hand were the Left parties, claiming to be solving urban problems, and on the other were groups of marginalised militants, sometimes advocating terrorism. Neither option particularly appealed to activists in the urban movements, which entered a period of sharp decline. Both Ceccarelli and Evers argue that to a large extent these activists were displaced into other more broadly based political activity – the peace movement, nuclear energy, abortion. Evers sums up the situation: 'In the last few years the struggles of immediate urban origin have fallen out of the limelight, to be replaced by movements for far more cultural autonomy . . . the organisations of the unemployed outside the factory, the Women's Movement' (Evers, 1981, p. 31). Moreover, those urban movements that do remain generally behave as conventional pressure groups, seeking legislative change or isolated reform.

Of all European countries Italy has had the most intense and pervasive experience or urban protest. An attempt has been made here to use the discussion to point out some of the complexities involved in the analysis of urban social movements in a country with, at one time, a high level of mobilisation, and why the movements faded. In France, despite the militancy of the students' and workers' movements in the late 1960s and early 1970s, urban protest was on a much lower and less threatening level. Evers suggests in relation to France, 'Rather than discussing a movement here, we should talk in terms of isolated "initiatives"' (Evers, 1981, p. 31). The focus mainly fell on the slum clearance schemes in Paris which displaced thousands of families into outlying modern developments, and a sustained protest movement based on the plight of immigrant workers living in squalid hostels. Rural/urban migration did not occur on anything like the same scale as Italy in the post-war decades. Most protest has instead focused on the redevelopment of Paris in the 1960s and 1970s. Major struggles involving technical and white-collar workers occurred at various stages in the construction of the Grandes Ensembles (see Castells, 1983, Part Two). As in Spain and Italy, the Left parties have controlled much of local government since the late 1970s and this has tended, as in the other countries, to dissipate the activity of urban movements. There is again evidence that some of this political energy has been absorbed into the peace campaign and, in France in particular, into new movements based on ecological issues. But the profile of urban political activity in France, compared either to Italy or to Spain, is very much lower, more segmented and isolated around a few specific issue bases.

It is clearly impossible to do more than hint at the complex range of factors relating to the growth and demise (at the present time) of urban movement activity. Something of the complexity within single nations has been indicated, and this in turn suggests that cross-national comparisons should be approached with caution. Some key structuring elements are, however, apparent:

1. A crucial area of relationship exists between urban movements and the formal party political system. In Italy, France and Spain urban social movements and urban protest largely collapsed in the face of widespread electoral success by the major left-wing parties in the mid- and late

1970s. Apart from defining precisely the terms of this interaction, the wider question here concerns the influence that urban movements had on these electoral successes: whether, in particular, urban protest anticipated and prepared the ground for the electoral victories.

2. There is clear evidence of the displacement of activists from urban movements into the peace movement, the ecological movement and other more broadly based political and cultural organisations.

3. In all three countries, particularly in Italy, there were important intra-national variations in timing, levels and types of urban mobilisations. Comparative analysts must face the problem that there may not be settled national patterns, especially in societies with historic territorial divisions.

4. The pattern of urban protest was to a large extent conditioned by social and demographic adaptations to the economic development of the nation. This has two main dimensions. First, the initial drive for rapid economic growth and industrialisation led to a period of rapid urbanisation, with mass relocation of population from rural to urban areas. State organisations both nationally and locally responded slowly to desperately inadequate infrastructure which led to the growth of shanty towns; this was particularly a problem for formerly non-industrialised cities and towns where the most militant urban protest tended initially to be focused. Second, in later phases of economic development (with a slowdown in the rates of growth, problems of over-production, and restructuring of industry towards more capital-intensive technologies) another more generalised phase of urban protest develops as issues of the 'social wage' become more significant relative to salary and wage levels.

5. The historic traditions of public administration and the politics of the local government systems exert an important influence on the way people respond to local issues.

6. There is evidence of a public/private sectoral influence on the structuring of key urban issues, particularly around transport and housing, and generally implying the differential enforcement of private property rights and private

interests against an undercapitalised and underfunded public sector with urban protest targeted against it.

The list indicates the important range of factors that may need to be considered in a comparative framework of analysis. But it is derived from sketches of only three countries, geographically adjacent, and with some historical and cultural heritage in common. In the next three sections societies with apparently very different political, economic and historical characteristics are considered.

An environmental movement in an East European socialist state

There are no records of urban social movements in Eastern bloc countries in the urban studies literature. Whether this is because urban protest does not exist or because it is not tolerated in bureaucratically deformed workers' states is unclear. A cross-cultural theory should at least attempt to account for this absence, but the research does not appear to have been done. Castells does not attempt to theorise this situation and has nothing to say about urban social change in socialist states, which account for approximately one-third of the world's population: 'In this book we have had to exclude analyses of the "state-planned societies" because of the absence of reliable data on urban movements in such a context' (Castells, 1983, p. xviii) This is somewhat incongruous, given the amount of space he devotes to discussing the role of Marx and Lenin in the historical process of class struggle and the ambiguities in classical Marxism over the existence of urban movements (Castells, 1983, pp. 298–9).

One recent case study on Poland offers an opportunity for an insight into the situation covering social movements in an Eastern bloc nation. It should be repeated that there are inherent dangers in generalising from case studies, especially those in which the circumstances are untypical.

The historical context against which an environmental movement developed in Poland in the late 1970s was the rise of the Solidarity trade union, but the organisation itself, the Polish Ecology Club (Polski Klub Ekologiczny, PKE) is a separate and independent body that survived the period of martial law and the curbs on Solidarity (Serafin, 1982). The environmental issue in Poland is based on the large-scale and highly destructive pollution created as a result of post-war industrialisation, in the context of a highly centralised state-planning machine. The pressure for growth was so intensive that, despite a con-stitutional commitment to control the development process, many basic environmental considerations were overridden or became snared in the bureaucratic administrative process. An early post-war example of the problems created by rapid industrialisation was the construction of the aluminium smelter at Skawina in Silesia. When it opened in 1954 it had an annual production of 15,000 tons, but by a series of extensions and forced production reached a figure of 53,000 tons in 1980. Serafin quotes a figure of an annual release into the atmosphere of the highly toxic fluorine compound of over 1000 tons; this has been responsible for crumbling facades of buildings in the historic city of Cracow and for poor harvests, and has con-stituted a danger to livestock and to humans. Serafin observes, 'To many, the Skawina Plant is a symbol of Poland's ecological crisis and, most important, of the direct links between that crisis and the misguided political and economic policies of post-war Polish planners' (Serafin, 1982, p. 178).

During the 1970s, under the leadership of Gierek, the drive for growth took on a new vigour, fuelled by massive borrowing on the international money markets, and the importation of Western technologies. The pollution control agencies were side-stepped as growth became essential in order to pay off foreign debt. By the end of the decade the environmental consequences were so severe that a report prepared for the State Environmen-tal Inspectorate indicated that a high proportion of Poland's rivers and lakes were effectively dead and air pollution was reaching crisis proportions. The report concludes, 'the danger of a biological catastrophe on a national scale is immediate if no action is taken now'. The report only came to light because of the activities of Solidarity, but concern for health and safety at work and environmental pollution was widespread as a result of direct experience, particularly in the major industrial centres. Solidarity's own research group reported to the 1981 congress of the union and their recommendations were passed unanimous-ly.

The widespread concern over, and experience of, industrial pollution was given an organisational expression with the establishment in September 1980 of the Polish Ecology Club. The founder members were shop stewards, journalists, doctors and academics concerned particularly about the environment of Cracow. Support for it grew rapidly, and by the spring of 1981 it had branches in all the main provincial centres. It was fundamentally a workers' movement, but drew support from many white-collar workers and professionals. It is a curiosity of comparative urban studies that one of the best examples of a 'pluriclass' social movement should occur in the People's Republic of Poland. PKE was officially registered in May 1981, and this formal recognition demonstrates how deeply worried the Polish authorities must be about the environmental issue. In many ways, PKE operates in the manner of a Western pressure group, with its own branches, meetings, research and campaigns. The most notable success was the role PKE played in the events leading up to the much publicised closure of the Skawina aluminium smelter in January 1981 (*The Economist*, 8 January 1981). This included a large-scale local campaign and a series of court actions against the managers of the plant by local people claiming compensation for damage to their health.

Although it is not clear from the available evidence, it seems certain that the Polish government, in recognition of the economic consequences of continued, large-scale pollution, have allowed PKE to act as a sounding-board over the environmental issue, and used its existence to legitimise their claims to be conscious of the problems and willing to act. Writing about Polish local councils, Piekalkiewicz observes:

> the skilful use of controlled popular participation and criticism within the framework of the councils provides the leadership with valuable channels of information and indoctrination. The criticism provides a safety valve for pressure which can be loosened up or tightened according to the leadership's evaluation of the situation. (Piekalkiewicz, 1975)

Given the monopoly of power wielded by the organs of the central state, much the same conclusion must be drawn concerning the existence of PKE. It exists through the tolerance of the government, representing a form of incorporation and co-option that is more blatant than it is often possible to achieve in West European states.

The background and conditions in which the environmental movement developed in Poland shares some similarities and some differences compared with the urban movements in Southern Europe. They all have in common the phenomenal period of post-war reconstruction based on a drive for economic growth through rapid industrialisation. Poland shared with Italy and Spain a period of rapid post-war rural-urban migration largely associated with industrialisation (Iwanicka-Lyra, 1972). But unlike the Western economies, which experienced largely uncontrolled drift to industrial centres, the 'planned' socialist economies had some influence on the timing and direction of the population movements. They very often produced sudden labour demands as a result of central decisions on industrial location, but avoided the worst problems of lack of housing and infrastructure through the planning machinery. As Cochrane argues,

> There have been major programmes of state spending on urban projects in Poland. The high-rise 'suburbs' of most Polish cities, the development of several new towns (including Nowa Huta) and the provision of the associated urban infrastructure should be enough to indicate that. Without Poland's particular state socialist structure it is difficult to believe that these developments, which have changed the face of major cities such as Cracow, would have taken place. (Cochrane, 1981, p. 204)

This is the first major difference between an Eastern bloc society and capitalist nations of Southern Europe (and the 'West' in general): urban protest has been avoided by the centrally directed development of the industrial and urban infrastructure. It is crucial to note that the Polish planners have invariably given industrial investment priority over social spending. This has created two important consequences for Polish society: first, the massive and uncontained environmental pollution of large tracts of the country; and second, it has led them to allow, or be unable to control, the growth of a private sector in the social consumption field, especially in housing provision (Ball and Harloe, 1974; see also Kenedi, undated, for an account of the private housing market in Hungary, and Musgrave, 1984, on Czechoslovakia). In the consumption sphere the differences between the Eastern and Western blocs may not be as great as the difference between the core industrial sector, where the conventional model of free market or mixed economies versus centralised state planning is predominately accurate.

Castells's suggestion on the fact that the urban inequalities in the two blocs have some similarities, and that 'this is due to the persistence of elements of the capitalist mode of development in the socialist states' (reported by Harloe, 1981, p. 186) is not an adequate response. It fails to theorise the historical and political experience of Eastern bloc societies by arguing for a 'persistence' thesis. The evidence suggests a more complex pattern of events in which the bureaucratic deformation of these states was accompanied by (and partly created by) the need for rapid industrialisation in the context of the global power of the capitalist bloc. Private enterprise was never specifically excluded and was overlaid not by the 'persistence' of capitalist 'elements' but by the privileged position of a powerful bureaucratic caste. The emergence of significant private sectors, especially in housing, but also in transport with the growth of significant levels of car ownership (Dunleavy, 1980) does not imply the re-emergence of 'capitalism' but of 'market' solutions to individual need and the problems of social consumption spending. As Janos Kenedi's book brilliantly illustrates, the private housing market is heavily dependent on the systematic corruption and buying of favours from within the bureaucratically managed state sector. The important relationships are therefore, first, between the dominant tendency of a drive for rapid industrialisation against the subordinate position of social consumption provision; and second, the dominance of a bureaucratically deformed and authoritarian state planning machine against a relatively small, weak and dependent private sector. Urban politics and the apparently low level of urban social movement activity in the Eastern bloc societies are structured by these key factors. This generally implies that the private sector is very individualistic – that is to say, it is dependent on the furtive building of contacts – and that the public sector is dominant through the state planning machinery, both factors working against social movement development unless on a regulated and co-opted basis in the public sector field. It may be that, in time, the adoption of market solutions in housing and other areas of consumption provision may lead to the emergence of social movements based on a public/private sectoral divide. In the West, the pattern and forms of control and mediation are more complex, involving a greater range of strategies of co-option and manipulation, but also vulnerability to socially created change.

We turn now to the opposite extreme from the Eastern bloc socialist states, to the free-market society of the United States of America.

Social movements in the United States of America

In contrast to the paucity of information on urban movements in the socialist states, there is an abundance of material to draw from in the USA. The problem, in this case, is to sift out the most useful for comparative purposes. Several recent studies of urban social movements in the USA have provided important insights into the factors that structure the American experience of urban social change. It is apparent from these that there are some exceptional features of the society that suggest great contrasts between the USA and the West and East European processes of urban movement development. The single most important difference concerns the black/white racial division, and for this reason we have chosen to concentrate on two social movements that centred on this core structuring element – the black schools movement and the inner-city riots of the 1960s. The racial divide in US society is additionally overlaid by two other central, historically determined features: the nature of the American class system and the structure of political power in the cities, both of which feed into the pattern of urban protest. This focus excludes a multiplicity of urban, cultural and social movements but does draw attention to core features in the comparative debate on urban politics, notably the race factor and the nature of corporate capitalism (compared to centralised state socialism).

In addition, the manner in which the class structure and 'meaning' systems have developed are distinctively contrasted with the West European experience of class. Of principal significance here is the absence of a mass labour movement in the USA, and an important division between the workplace and the home environment in people's perception of class. As Katznelson argues,

> American urban politics has been governed by boundaries and rules that stress ethnicity, race and territoriality, rather than class, and that emphasize the distribution of goods and services, while excluding questions of production or workplace relations. *The centerpiece of these rules has been the radical separation in people's consciousness, speech, and activity of the politics of work from the politics of community.* (Katznelson, 1981, p. 6).

He goes on to argue that it is only possible to understand urban movements if they are correctly located in their social and historical contexts. He has studied the political culture of the US working class as a prerequisite to making sense of the urban movements of the 1960s.

The schools movement

In a later article Katznelson, with Gille and Weir, goes on to argue that the type of analytical position outlined above must be part of the comparative study of urban movements: 'In cross-national perspective both the relevant policies and groups vary from society to society, even if they share in broad constraints dictated by the logic of the mode of production' (Katznelson, Gille and Weir, 1982, p. 222). This leads them to discuss a case study of a core urban movement in US society, the struggle for black public schooling. Here, the history of state intervention into the provision of schooling followed a pattern that was specific to America. In short, education was widely considered by most social strata to be a right of people in a free society. Early demands for education were not subject, therefore, to a class-defined political struggle. The contrast with the situation in England in the late nineteenth century is striking: workers were excluded from access to elementary schooling so that, when the 1870 Education Act was eventually passed, the terms of educational provision in the society were indelibly imprinted by their class-defined exclusion; because of their subordinate position, the working class were unable to stop the educational system – particularly at secondary level – developing on a class-divided pattern. For the white US working class, full citizenship had already been established and it was assumed that access to mass schooling, and to a say in how it should develop, was automatic. For blacks, however, the same guarantee of influence did not exist.

The school systems, particularly in the southern states, divided on racial grounds with strict codes prohibiting mixing. But because education was so central a tenet of citizenship of the society the black community 'tirelessly searched for new ways to influence school policy' (p. 225). It was a core issue in the growth of a unified black movement in both the southern and northern states. The important point in the context of US politics was that the schools issue generated political responses fundamentally dependent on racial and not class criteria. As Katznelson, Gille and Weir suggest, 'In the area of schooling in the United States, the relevant linkages muted class but highlighted race as bases of collective action' (p. 230). They go on to argue that even the terms on which incorporation was eventually based tended to highlight the blacks as a distinct economic, cultural and political section of the society. This in turn created the boundaries for the whole urban black movement, specifically isolating them from the white US working class.

The treatment of US urban movements must, therefore, be sensitive to a range of factors unique to the country. Katznelson talks of an 'American exceptionalism' thesis built around key features of a non-class-defined social system. These range not simply across the absence of a working-class movement, but is crucially related to the schooling history in the context of a weak welfare state: that is to say, compared to many European systems, the American system showed the early formation of open, public schooling provision (arising from the terms of US citizenship), counter-balanced by a very belated and fragmentary system of social insurance and public services. Second, the historical context of US working-class politics has been conditioned by 'a pattern of class formation marked above all by a stark divide between a consciousness and a politics of work and off-work. Off work, in their residential communities, American workers have acted mainly on the basis of nonclass territorial and ethnic affiliations' (Katznelson, Gille and Weir, 1982, p. 231). Third, for blacks both the 'high-schooling, low social welfare' conditioning and the 'work, off-work' situation have had less of an impact than their structural/historical exclusion from the terms of the dominant white society. Racism cross-cuts US society. The analysis of all urban movements in the USA needs to be seen against these 'exceptional' tenets of the society.

These themes can be traced in the numerous analyses of the black riots of the 1960s, but it is only recently that these social movements have been located in the context of the political power systems that structure city politics in the USA. It is the identification of this power system and its influence on the level and intensity of the rioting that has recently been made by Friedland (1982). This adds a crucial element to the analytical propositions for the study of urban social movements in US society in relation to the nature of city power, and the ways in which this interacted with the black ghetto riots.

City power and race riots

Friedland adopts what he calls a 'structural' perspective for the analysis of urban political power. By this he means that the policy initiatives and practice in US cities are crucially influenced by the presence or absence of key organisations. In this he is arguing a line of thought associated in European political studies with the work of Lukes, whose work on the silent exercise of political power by dominant interests is seen as increasingly influential (Lukes, 1975). In the US context Friedland describes the influence both of large industrial corporations and of large trade unions on the structuring and patterning of urban policy. He shows that the existence of strong or weak corporate and/or union organisation in specific cities decisively affected the shape of core policy, and exemplifies this by an examination of the urban renewal strategies and War on Poverty programmes commonly adopted in US cities in the late 1960s and 1970s. He argues, for example, that 'cities respond to the War on Poverty not because of the local level of poverty per se, but because that poverty – its extent and its color – threatened local corporate and union power' (Friedland, 1982). In later chapters in the book Friedland examines the black ghetto riots in the context of this model by re-working statistical data collected by Spilerman (Spilerman, 1970, 1971, 1974) on the extent and intensity of the riots.

The mid-1960s witnessed massive, often very violent, black riots in all the major cities of the USA. Over 300 serious riots are recorded between 1964 and 1968, with a peak (with three-quarters of the main riots) in 1967 and 1968. At least 300 people were killed. Following on from the Civil Rights Movement of the early 1960s, new demands had emerged; demands not just for recognition in a society that had been closed to blacks, but for some share in its fruits – jobs, housing, open educational competition. The riots occurred as a response of desperate and effectively disenfranchised communities which were often leaderless, having lost their most effective leaders to employment in the community programmes.

The face of city politics was dramatically restructured by the riots. There were two major consequences. First, black mayors, for the first time, were elected in dozens of cities and blacks took part in city councils and all the procedural and administrative committees. The effect of this was to increase welfare budgets and to limit the growth of the city bureaucracies. Second, as Friedland argues, 'as city government scrambled to deliver more services and more jobs to blacks, calls for "law and order" became deafening. Cities stock-piled riot technology' (Friedland, 1982, p. 168). Friedland goes on to argue that the underlying issue for government in the post-riot phase was to balance the extent of concessions against the danger of stimulating more riots. This calculation also involved the extent of repression that could be employed 'to enforce the limits of reform' without itself creating new resistance. In the event both strategies were used in the hope that some sort of balance between reform and repression could be struck.

One of the important findings from this analysis is the rationality of rioting as a political tactic geared towards the production of jobs, services and power shifts. Friedland shows that the severity of the riots correlated strongly with a range of variables – non-white population size, demand for low-rent housing, poverty funding, urban renewal activity, police activity and non-reformed local government. Severity of riots was not arbitrary, but was conditioned by specific sets of factors. Cities with large urban renewal programmes had intense political violence: 'Urban renewal was a visible indicator of the city's commitment to displace the black community, to woo a whiter, wealthier clientele' (Friedland, 1982, p. 162). The poverty programme also caused intense violence, by providing only limited access for blacks to jobs and local power. Having ignited this potential and absorbed some of the best leadership, the poverty programme totally failed to meet the rising tide of expectations, especially among young blacks. As Friedland poignantly remarks, 'A routine arrest, an explosion' (1982, p. 163). Riot severity was, therefore, closely linked to urban renewal and the poverty programme, but riot *frequency* was not. This is because, if rioting was a strategy that aimed to win benefits, then controlling outbreaks of new violence would be necessary in order to capitalise on the initial outburst – in the form of jobs, services and the extension of power to blacks. As Friedland suggests, 'From this perspective, that public policies have less effect on the local number of riots than they do on the aggregate severity of riot activity would not be unexpected' (1982, p. 163).

The crucial factor in the pattern of settlement was the nature of the power relationship between on the one hand black electoral influence and black violence, and on the other the nature of the city interests threatened, revolving, Friedland argues, around the existence or absence of corporate and union influences in the city power structure. He found a very positive correlation between responses (to the riots) using patronage and co-optive strategies in corporate or union-dominated cities, and the use only of repressive tactics in non-corporate/non-union cities. In these types of cities, political power is structured by the conservative influence of small-scale employers using non-union labour. 'Thus whether political violence sparks an expansion of the public pork barrel depends on the class composition of local political power' (Friedland, 1982), p. 178).

Moreover, the structuring of power in corporate or union-dominated cities and the treatment of the blacks was also differentially related. Because the labour interest is tied to electoral support through the Democratic Party, cities with a high union influence reacted both with patronage to the black community and repression. In weak union cities blacks confronted only repression. The corporate influence was, however, ideologically opposed to welfare solutions and not dependent on the numerical support of blacks at the ballot box. For this reason the only way to wrest concessions from corporate cities was through violence. Friedland concludes:

> Corporations can invest or not invest, thereby encouraging the city to do their bidding. Labour unions must rely on their leverage at the polls . . . Black numbers, especially volatile black numbers, threatened these bases of union power. Then, like an ambivalent lover, the unions came down on the blacks with both concessions and fists. (Friedland, 1982, p. 179)

Friedland's general argument, that power can be wielded through invisible, powerful and subtle influences – in this case by the presence of union and corporate interests in US cities – is an (unacknowledged) extension of a European tradition of power studies (Lukes, 1975; Dunleavy, 1977; Saunders, 1979). But as Darke (1983) points out, it stands at the end of a long tradition of community power studies in the US urban politics literature. As a structural model it is particularly important because Friedland has demonstrated, in the case of the incidence and intensity of black riots, and crucially the responses to them, that the presence or absence of certain types of economic and political interests have determined certain types of policy output. Some influences can 'shape public policy without speaking' (Friedland, 1982, p. 210).

There are important lessons in this case study for the analysis of urban social movements. The key point is that any analysis or interpretation of a social movement must be read in the context of the type of local political system within which it operates, *and* that the major determinants of local power are nationally structured economic and ideological interests. This is the case whether we are considering a free-market Western society or an Eastern bloc deformed socialist state. The context of US society is much more complex because of the intricate patterning of the social and political systems that is structured along a number of crucial lines of cleavage – black versus white, a complex class structure, and reformed and unreformed local government.

Moreover, the faces of political power are often less visible until they are provoked into action. Most important of all, the sources of power, in large and small-scale industrial and financial interests, are mediated by the city's political systems. The bureaucratically deformed workers' states of Eastern Europe do not share this plurality of influences and these intricate systems of social control. As we have seen, centralised state power is the absolutely dominant and unmediated force. This monopoly of power is based on a totally nationalised industrial economy (with the exception of the housing sector), state control of information and the media, and repression. In these societies urban movements do not exist because they are not allowed to exist. In the USA social control must operate through more subtle processes of co-option and repression, but the sources of power are equally dominant and the state machine is equally prepared for violent repression. The tactic of reformism is the single greatest difference between the two societies: the one possesses it, the other does not and does not need to.

We turn now to types of society in which the theme of dependency and domination are equally pervasive but with different costs and consequences in urban politics. These are the countries of the so-called 'Third World', which, in reality, are intimately linked to the economic and political interests of the major world power blocs. Often they are societies in the throes of a rapid urbanisation process, creating high levels of rural-urban migration. Many of these migrants and new arrivals live in the peripheral shanty towns surrounding the main cities. The existence of these marginalised people has come to define the image of the Third World city, and in important ways structures its economy. And these peripheral communities are the social base of a profusion of urban social movements.

The shanty-towns of South America

It has been estimated that as much as one-tenth of the world's population lives in urban squatting and shanty town communities (Gimson, 1980). Virtually every major centre of population in Africa, Asia and South America has shanty town dwellers to a greater or lesser degree. It is common for 30–40 per cent of the population of major cities in these areas to live in illegally sited shelters and shacks; in some instances it can be much higher: Addis Abbaba 90 per cent (1968); Mombasa 66 per cent (1970); Ibadan 75 per cent (1971); Kinshasa 60 per cent (1969); Rabat 60 per cent (1971); Bogota 60 per cent (1970); Mexico City 46 per cent (1970); Chimbote (Peru) 67 per cent (1970) (Castells, 1983, p. 178).

A brief discussion of this phenomenon is included partly because of its sheer scale, but primarily because an important range of comparative themes arises from the types of urban movement generated in these vast peripheral communities. What kind of movements develop? What are their demands and characteristics?

The existing case studies indicate a great diversity of movements based on shanty town communities. The core issue is obviously the right to invade and occupy peripheral land. Once established, demands may then develop for the provision of urban services or more permanent accommodation. Furthermore, given the somewhat tenuous legal attachment to the sites, movements often emerge to defend their territory from the plans of urban developers. Within the same city at the same time several of these types of issues may generate urban movements. The dominant themes that structure these organisations concern their dependent relationship to the state. Castells's perceptive analysis of this point will be described later in the section. To illustrate the types of movement that develop, reference is made to two case studies: the settlement struggle (*colonias de lucha*) in the Mexican city of Monterrey (taken from Castells) and a movement against an urban development scheme in the shanty town zone of Bogota (*barrios populares*) (Janssen, 1978).

The origins of the Monterrey squatters' movement is in the history of a gradually expanding and not unprosperous city based on an important steel industry. But the consequences of industrial growth and the mechanisation of farming produced large-scale immigration with a demand for housing that was impossible to fulfil. As a result, 300,000 people live as squatters in the city (Castells, 1983, p. 197). The settlement struggles began as the result of student intervention to extend the limited and speculative control by the public administrators of the squatter territories. The first new settlement provoked violent police reaction, but after several months they withdrew and the area became established. Other new settlements were established by tactically astute exploitation of political splits between dominant economic interests and the government. Castells quotes the example of the conflict between Monterrey's influential and conservative bourgeoisie and the reformism of President Echeverria: 'Using the themes of the governor's populist speeches as justification of their actions, the squatters made open repression against them more difficult' (Castells, 1983, p. 197). In the backlash against them, provoked by the local elites, the police killed six squatters. This outrage generated massive demonstrations, linking squatters, students and workers; the police chief in Monterrey was ousted and financial support was given by the government to support the squatters' settlement. But the level of politicisation in this movement was such that they rejected most offers of state aid or legal recognition, arguing instead that their autonomy was more important.

The settlements developed their own infrastructure – schools, clinics, roads – and illegally connected themselves to the water and sanitary services of the city. Despite this advanced and high level of organisation and consciousness, the movement was isolated from mainstream society because it was composed mainly of unemployed people or migrant peasants and had no connections with the workers' movement in the city. The settlements were vulnerable to repression (by the army) and to their own political infighting. The movement shows, however, that despite the very marginalised status of 'unofficial' squatting, it was possible for squatters' movements to maintain a high degree of autonomy by playing on the internal contradictions of the state.

> Ultimately, however, it was not possible to remain outside the social system and, in particular, in order to sustain what was effectively a change in urban 'meaning' (from bourgeoisie domination to co-operative living) the movement is dependent on changes in the wider political system. This was a role played by the Chilean squatters during the period of Allende's Popular Unity government, by becoming a focal point for a range of social strata involved in the attempt to transform the society. (Castells, 1983, pp. 199–209)

In the case of the Monterrey squatter settlements their autonomy was built in an unlinked political vacuum and so was vulnerable.

The process by which squatter communities are co-opted and manipulated by the dominant political and economic forces is also seen in the struggle of the shanty town (*barrios*) dwellers of Bogota against a large-scale urban renewal scheme. In this case the delays caused by the movement did cause some changes to the project. But the significant evidence concerns the divisions that existed within the social structure of the *barrios* community between squatters, small businessmen and individual dwelling owners which the city machine was able to exploit.

The plan was for a redevelopment including an eleven kilometre stretch of six-lane motorway going through the eastern *barrios* area. The sponsors and major interest groups behind the scheme were politicians (often involved with construction companies), speculative landowners and a number of finance corporations. Fifty per cent of the finance was to come from the USA. A number of *barrios* committees were established to oppose the plan (popularly called '*Plan de los Semuchos*', or the 'bribery plan'), and managed to impede attempts to clear families. For several years the *barrios* committees united to oppose the plan but a harder line approach by the city authorities weakened their resolve. Individual home-owners were offered good compensation, and some who worked for the city administration were threatened with dismissal. By a gradual process of manipulation the solidarity of the *barrios* areas weakened. Some eighty houses were demolished as the first stage of implementing the plan.

Doubts about the technical and financial basis of the scheme had become widespread, and following the presidential elections the new Liberal president withdrew government support for the original plan and put forward a much smaller alternative, including a ring road. The *barrios* committees had thus caused sufficient delay for the scheme to be dropped; they had united the disparate and disunited *barrios* dwellers. In the end their unity was broken by the city and development interests, who divided their ranks along social and ownership lines. There was a basic conflict of interest between owners, tenants and squatters. As Janssen suggests, 'Because their interests can be opposed in the short term, the unity of any movement can be undermined' (Janssen, 1978, p. 158).

The fundamental point is that all these urban developments, even if they are described as 'peripheral', are in fact a core element in the urban structure of Third World cities. But the social relationships they express are crucially those of dependency. This is the thrust of Castells's analysis of squatters in Latin America. The nation states of the area are caught between a series of conflicting pressures generated by their indigenous, traditional oligarchies, and the intervention of multinational corporations in the modernising process. As part of the process of adapting to and controlling these forces, particularly in negotiating or re-negotiating their way out of dependency on foreign investment, the shanty town communities have a particular role. As Castells suggests, 'Urban squatters appear as a target social group, potentially able to be both solicited and mobilized by the new, modernizing state institutions' (1983, p. 210). The squatters exist only in the context of a dependent relationship with the national states who are able to control them either by repression or co-option. 'Without the state's tolerance, or without some effective political support, they would not have the right to their physical presence in the city' (p. 211).

The second feature of this relationship and its territorial dimension relates to the economic function that the shanty towns perform. At its simplest, this involves the low cost reproduction of labour power which, in turn, allows for a more profitable exploitation of the economy by international capital or by the state itself. The consequence of this for the urban structure is the spatial layout of the shanty towns, allowing for small-scale subsistence cultivation. High-rise, flatted accommodation would be highly inappropriate in the context of this economic process. Around this territorial unit a complex 'informal' economy develops – of small repair shops, drugs, building contractors – which forms an unofficial but crucial element of the urban economy.

The squatter settlements of the Third World exist at the end of a chain of dependencies. Their territorial extent, their relationship to the state and the informal economy all merge to produce what Castells calls 'the dependent city'. In it the people are responsible for their own welfare and, for them to do so, the state must disregard its institutional rules.

The dependent city is the ecological form resulting from the residents' lack of social control over urban development because of their forced submission to the good will of the state and to the changing flows of foreign capital. The dependent city is a city without citizens. (Castells, 1983, p. 212)

Models for comparing urban social movements

In the opening section of this chapter the controversy over the interpretation of the scale and stage of development of urban social movements in Europe and across the globe as a whole was noted. Castells's notion of an upswing of activity was criticised, because he has upheld this position despite evidence to the contrary. Castells's position may reflect his theoretical emphasis on the 'urban' as the source of social change, so that the upswing thesis is consequent upon his theoretical propositions. Similar problems with his general 'cross-cultural theory of urban social change' were identified in Chapter 2; in particular, that his use of the Madrid Citizens' Movement as the archetypal urban social movement is an untenable empirical and theoretical position, given the circumstances of its development and demise, and the insufficient evidence to support his claims for it, especially in the 'community/cultural' dimension. Nevertheless, Castells has constructed a model for urban social change (the elements of which we described in Chapter 2) which is effectively an attempt at an all-embracing, unitary theory of comparative urban social movements. As Pickvance suggests, 'For our purpose, what is crucial abaout Castells's analysis in *The City and the Grassroots* is that it seeks to deal with the diversity of urban movement experience by means of a *single model applying to all cases*' (Pickvance, 1983, p. 3). Pickvance rejects Castells's model as a repetition of the early position in which urban social movements were defined by a range of specific characteristics. In the new definition the idea of an exclusive framework based on an archetypal model (in the earlier case, the Chilean squatters' movement) is replicated but with a different set of analytical criteria.

Pickvance goes on to propose an alternative model for the comparative analysis of urban social movements. His ideas contain some useful pointers to how a comparative approach might proceed. Despite his emphasis on diversity, problems arise because it too is a structural model dependent on the identification of key variables.

As with Castells's theory, the modelling produces a wrong emphasis: one in which attention focuses on the internal logic of the model rather than on the causal analysis of urban movements and on the field of the urban political process, which should be the *raison d'être* for the focus on urban movements. This view is closer to Castells's recent position in suggesting that urban movements are crucial signposts of the political system, but (unike Castells) provide avenues to the key areas of non-protest, the invisible faces of power, and the important arena of interaction between urban conflict and political parties.

In his model, Pickvance describes four main influences that affect the existence and characteristics of urban movements in different countries. He also proposes a typology of urban movements, based on existing empirical data, and suggests that it is possible to predict the likely existence of particular types of movement from the societal features he has identified.

The first feature Pickvance highlights is rapid urbanisation, which is associated with demands for the provision of basic urban services and housing. Examples here include the squatter movements of the Third World cities. The second societal element that may lead to urban movements is the intervention of the state in the consumption arena, i.e. the politicisation of the urban initially identified by Castells. Examples of types of movement generated by this factor are abundant, and often concern issues of access to facilities – council houses, public transport, libraries. Also under this heading are movements seeking greater control and management rights over the public provision of services, and movements acting to defend their property from state activity in urban renewal and redevelopment. The third feature outlined by Pickvance is whether the formal political institutions enable discontent to be voiced. This he specifically relates to the existence, or not, of opposition political parties; he predicts an inverse relationship between the expression of protest through effective opposition parties and the extent of urban movement activity. Pickvance points here to the Spanish neighbourhood movement, at the end of the Franquist era, and also the collapse, as we have seen, of urban movements in France and Italy with the success of Left parties in local government in the late 1970s. The final societal feature is described as 'general economic and social conditions' (p. 5). Periods of economic crisis tend to lead to the decline of movements seeking state spending and those defending themselves from state activity as renewal programmes are suspended or cancelled. Conditions of 'social tension and raised expectations', on the other hand, lead to a rise of movements seeking popular control and management of services.

Pickvance's models are useful as illustrations of many of the factors involved in the comparative analysis of urban social movements. In particular they show the major societal conditions under which certain types of movement might be expected to develop. It is in drawing attention to factors such as the effectiveness of the political institutions in expressing social conflict, or in phases of rapid urbanisation, that we can begin to account for varying levels of urban movement activity across the globe. But the attempt to sustain a logically consistent set of models on the basis of the identification of key societal elements potentially has the same drawback as Castells's unitary theory: the initial definition of factors to be considered prescribes the scope of the analysis.

The suggestion here is not for an alternative model but a number of key propositions about the causal mechanisms of urban movement mobilisation. These include some of the elements from Pickvance's material, but argues for an expanded range of themes. Cross-national comparisons may be facilitated by both a modelling and a thematic approach. Neither is mutually exclusive, and an emphasis on a plurality of methodologies may be more illuminating than a single model at this still relatively immature stage of comparative analysis. Pickvance's model seeks to account for a particular problem – the lull/upswing contradiction – and this has created an emphasis on the scale and timing of movement activity leading to a predictive model. This is an important area of debate, but there are other analytical themes which this approach does not consider or obscures. These are best indicated in relation to a number of specific problems in Pickvance's paper.

A central difficulty with his procedure arises from the structural method adopted: the linking of key societal features to certain types of movement. The problem here is whether the model adequately explains the relationship between the specified societal features, and the existence of certain types of urban movement. Moreover, Pickvance not only links movement existence to societal features, but claims to predict their existence: 'The logic of our argument has been that societies which share positions on the four societal dimensions *should have the same movement experience*, other things being equal' (p. 6, emphasis added). His illustrations, mainly drawn from Western Europe, do provide examples that suggest a 'fit' between movements and societal conditions, but this evidence simply indicates that his predictions have been given the appearance of *post hoc* verification.

The model is so open-ended that it can 'explain' a wide diversity of movement existence. For example, the suburbanisation of Paris in the post-war period (rapid urbanisation) led to movements demanding access to consumption facilities rather than demand movements for the provision of services, as the model would predict. Pickvance says that 'this is best seen as a demand for facilities already in existence elsewhere' (p. 7). Or where explanation appears to be impossible, the example becomes an 'exception'. For example, he argues that in countries where the working class has been integrated into power for lengthy periods, there will be lower levels of urban protest (under the heading of the effectiveness of political institutions in expressing social conflict). But Pickvance acknowledges under this head the exceptionality of the USA (p. 7).

In short, the model is not able to explain, for example, the black ghetto riots of the 1960s. The problem is that if we treat major societies such as the USA as exceptions (or, with Castells, the Eastern bloc socialist states) the comparative validity of the modelling process is tarnished. Pickvance does indicate that the empirical support for his thesis is based on Western Europe, but he clearly intends to suggest a global frame of reference – or, at least, a frame of reference covering both developed and developing societies. Pickvance has indentified some of the core themes in the analysis of comparative urban movements, but the causal links have not been sufficiently grounded.

These linkages are, however, crucial to the presence or *absence* and characteristics of urban movements. (Indeed, Pickvance acknowledges this theme at the end of his paper when he says that his approach 'leaves open an intriguing question: whether these general processes are limited to "hard" structural features of societies . . . or whether they include "softer" structural

182 Urban Social Movements

features, such as "cultural understandings"' (p. 9).) The word 'absence' is stressed here because Pickvance's models, while attempting to account for the lull of movement activity in recent years, is an action-centred model. It does not account for the analytically important theme of non-action. As Harloe observes, 'one cannot necessarily conclude that exclusion leaves no "clue" which can provide reasonable evidence of excluded alternatives and a basis for studying ways in which their exclusion occurred' (Harloe, 1981, p. 190). It has been suggested in Chapter 3, and in the case studies, that the sociology of urban movement social bases and the ideological structuring of the local political environment are two main influences on the process of exclusion. These are important causal mechanisms in the mobilisation process. But the theme of non-action/exclusion also leads to a core analytical field – of the nature and influence of corporate and state power acting to incorporate, marginalise or repress urban conflict.

Two key facets of a 'non-action' frame have been established. First, the pathfinding analysis of Friedland of the urban power structure in the USA shows beyond doubt that the mere presence or absence of key political actors – industrial corporations or large trade unions – decisively affected the patterning of responses to core public policy and to the black ghetto riots; that the scale and intensity of the black riots can *only* be understood in relation to the invisible faces of power in the city's political systems. As we observed, this is in line with a European school of thought on the nature of political power based on the work of Lukes. Strategies of co-option and repression used by the state to contain urban conflict are underpinned by specific forms of economic and political interests. In comparative studies this analytical field is a major theme. The high levels of urban conflict in the USA is not, therefore, an 'exception', but should be read as the consequence of a particular form of political power.

The same argument can be used in a second facet of the non-action frame discussed in the chapter, namely the question of the absence of urban protest in the Eastern bloc socialist states. Here the state system takes on a less mediated form, and we have argued that the buraucratic and centralised state planning machine is able to plan urban infrastructural development more directively than in the capitalist economies, and repressively contains non-legitimised social protest. The absence of urban social movements in the Eastern bloc – an apparent case of non-action – requires explanation not simply for completeness of coverage but because there are major theoretical and empirical comparative issues to be faced: some similarities in urban inequality, the linking of the economies of the Eastern bloc to Western capital, the nature of deformed socialist state systems, and the emergence of private sectors in the social consumption arena in Eastern bloc countries.

Changing the focus away from international comparisons, there is also a difficulty of interpretation and usage with Pickvance's model on an intra-national level. On a cross-national basis Pickvance predicts that in societies where 'the alternation of power of left and right parties in power centrally and locally is established', there will be lower levels of urban protest. He quotes Britain as an example. But, as indicated earlier, a large majority of the population in Britain lives in local authority areas where alternation between the parties is non-existent. In that case deductively we should be predicting higher levels of urban conflict in Britain than appears to be the case, and also a higher level of movement activity in the one-party areas compared to the cities and towns where political control of local councils does alternate between the parties. There is no firm evidence to support this contention, but it seems likely that there is no differential *level* of urban movement activity that could be ascribed to whether the authority is controlled by one party or is marginal. In Birmingham, for example, the major urban centre in Britain where political control regularly changes hands, there is ample evidence of urban protest and local movement activity (Newton, 1976; Fujishin, 1976; Lambert, Paris and Blackaby, 1978).

More important than arguments about levels of activity is the strong probability that the existence of 'one-party' local authorities does affect the types and strategies of protest movements, depending on whether control is in the hands of Labour or the Conservatives. For example, the ratepayer movement is closely identified with areas of long-term Labour control (see Chapter 5), or the reception given to council house tenants' movements generally gives rise to strategies of co-option or marginalisation depending on the political complexion of the local council (see Chapter 4; Saunders, 1979). Urban social movement activity is partially structured by the character of local political systems, leading to intra-national variations in movement types and strategies.

To sum up, as the basis of a comparative analysis of urban movement activity Pickvance's models outline some of the core structuring elements – rapid urbanisation, state intervention into social consumption provision, the effectiveness of political institutions in expressing political conflict, and a range of general economic and social conditions. There are drawbacks in the attempt to use these key societal elements as a predictive model, although it is recognised that Pickvance was developing his ideas in relation to a specific issue – the 'upswing/lull' debate. The models do not adequately explain the causal relationships between movement types and societal features, and that this leads to a number of difficulties; the models do not account for the non-action field with its important focus on the nature of urban power structures, and that there is a related problem involving the interpretation of which societies are seminal to the models and which are exceptional; and, finally, they do not acknowledge the existence of intra-national variations in urban movement types and activity.

Conclusion

There are a number of problems with a modelling methodology applied to the comparative analysis of urban social movements, both in the case of Castells's 'cross-cultural theory of urban social change' and Pickvance's models of 'diverse reality'. The difficulties are due to the structuring that is necessary in order to produce a logically consistent argument. These procedures can generate obscurity as well as illuminating reality. Our method, while not rejecting some of the substantive content of the models, argues for a more thematic approach. In the first instance the focus must be on the mobilisation process: the arena of action and non-action. From the case studies a range of themes can be identified, broadly classifiable under two headings: those relating to political process, and those relating to social process. Our suggestion is that the urban movement experience of each society needs to be read against those core influences.

Under the heading of *political process*, consideration must be made of:

1. The structure and political history of the local administrative system and its interaction with the central level – the theme of central/local relations.
2. The party political system in the society and its effectiveness in mediating social conflict. (This is essentially the same as Pickvance's notion of the ability of formal political institutions to express political conflict.)
3. The osmosis of activists between urban movements and the party system, and also the existence of social movements in the wider cultural/political sphere creating alternative sources of activism.
4. The identification of those economic and social forces that underpin the national and local state. The presence or absence of which decisively affects the policy strategies of the local authorities; and the tactical range available to urban protest movements.
5. The need to be sensitive to intra-national variations in urban movement experience.

The second group of comparative themes taken under the heading *socio-economic process* mainly concern the characteristics of the social bases from which movement activity might be generated or contained. The major facets here are:

1. The stage of development of the urbanisation process linked specifically to the periodisation of industrial production – of expansion or of decline, both potentially including economic and technological restructuring. Crucial to this theme is the role of the consumption process in assisting the restructuring of fundamental social and economic systems by providing new markets for goods, and in the ideological stabilisation of rapidly changing societies.
2. Closely linked to the latter processes is a set of considerations relating to social and demographic adaptations to national economic development. Periods of rural/urban migration may be involved here, but in the contemporary period a major source of social base production centres on the interface between the public and private sector provision of

social consumption, and generally involves a gradient of influences favourable to the private sector (although this has not yet assumed sufficient proportions likely to stimulate mobilisation in the Eastern bloc societies).

3. The sociology of the social bases requires close scrutiny: on the one hand, scrutiny of the range of mediating associational and social network factors that might screen out protest; and, on the other hand, of the identification of solidaristic communities based on residence or on common access to a service, both of which might generate a social movement.

This list is by no means closed, but it does contain the range of themes, identified in the case studies and in our evaluation of Castells's and Pickvance's comparative models, that may be purposefully employed in comparing urban social movements in different societies. The point is not to account for the unique experience of each nation but to indicate the core themes that underpin urban movement activity, leading to future refinements of analytical method and an illumination of social reality.

Chapter 7

The Theory and Practice of Urban Social Movements

The book has assembled a variety of evidence from Britain and other countries to describe and locate the place in urban political sociology of a range of organisations identified as urban social movements. It has been argued that this field of study offers important lines of approach to some of the most difficult and invariant issues in political studies: the influence of social movements on policy change, the factors that mediate and control social conflict, the sources of urban political power, the repercussions of the growth of social cleavages based on sectoral and modal shifts in consumption provision. Evidence from major types of society has been reviewed to illuminate the problems of whether there are any general urban processes or urban themes that can be identified through the analysis of comparative urban social movements, and whether the idea of modelling is an appropriate methodology for approaching cross-national analysis. Because of the seminal influence of Castells on the field of urban political sociology and his theoretical stance in relation to the role of urban movements, the material has been developed around a critique and appreciation of his work. It now remains to make a final assessment of the position Castells now adopts on the political significance of his urban social movements thesis, to summarise our theoretical approach, and to conclude with an evaluation of the place of urban movements in Britain in the 1980s.

Castells's new urban social movements

In Chapter 1 we pinpointed Castells's 'phase two' work as being potentially his most fruitful period. It was suggested that his identification of consumption cleavages that were independent of social class opened up a major new vein in urban studies. It has led, for example, to the important contribution made in recent years by Dunleavy, who initially sought to refine the concept of collective consumption into a workable subject field, and has subsequently gone on to identify the notion of socialised consumption as a response of Western economies to the structural problems of over-production.

In this middle period Castells's readjustment of the political strategies necessary for an effective urban social movement also harbours important lessons for the contemporary stage of urban politics. Later in Chapter 1, it was argued that the strategy of linking urban movements into a wider alliance of progressive, democratic forces is where the major current of urban politics in Britain in the mid-1980s is found. This is not a replication of Castells's position but a development from it. Indeed, there are important interpretative difficulties with the phase two specification of urban social movements. He argued, at that stage, for the significance of urban social movements in forging alliances between 'the new petty bourgeoisie' and the working class: 'The purpose is to go forward by controlling state institutions through democratic means (*essentially electoral ones*)' (Castells, 1978, p. 172, emphasis added). As argued in Chapter 2, this position must be read in the light of the election successes of the Communist Party in Italy, France and Spain in the mid-1970s. Castells sees urban social movements as paving the way for these victories and in anticipation of events yet to unfold ('the transformation of social relations').

The problem with this perspective is that urban social movements, in Castells's parlance, at once lose their strategic role at the front line of social change. They cease to be vanguard organisations and are, instead, seen as part of a gradualist infiltration of the state and as organisers of electoral tactics. In short, fundamental social change no longer depends directly on urban social movements, and so the significance of the urban contradiction is diminished. In practice, the Eurocommunist project has not led to the transformation of class forces; rather, the lessons of the 1980s are those relating to retrenchment and the consolidation of dominant class interests. As Ceccarelli argues, urban social movements in the 1970s may not have been the heralds of a new era, or indeed have anticipated the electoral successes of the Left. They were, instead, the symptoms of a process of social readjustment:

> It is possible that urban social movements and the conflicts which accompanied them, far from anticipating a new era, were the expression of the last and most conflictive stage of a process of change and readjustment to it. (Ceccarelli, 1982, p. 264)

This interpretation of urban social movements in Southern European politics in the 1970s is very different from that argued by Castells. There are two main points to be made. First, Ceccarelli's reading is made in the context of explaining the rapid decline of urban protest in the late 1970s, so that his account does have the advantage of hindsight and he is able to give a detailed reasoning of the events. Castells's response, on the other hand, as we saw, still holds to an 'upswing' thesis, albeit on a global rather than a European scale. He has answered the empirical dilemma by adopting a new view of the centrality of urban movements in contemporary society and not by resolving the problems of the Eurocommunist position.

Second, Ceccarelli's cautioning strongly suggests that urban social movements should not always, by definition, be seen as creators of social change. As we have suggested, there is an area of tactical ambiguity in Castells' middle phase, because urban social movements no longer appear to be the instruments of social transformation. Moreover, in the phase three position, not only is this issue not resolved but in some respects it is even more incongruous. As we saw in Chapter 1, Castells restates, in *The City and the Grassroots*, the centrality of the urban as the source of social change, but he does not explain his switch from 'broad Left' politics to the adoption of 'alternative' cultural and political strategies, which specifically *excludes* joint action between urban social movements and political parties. Indeed, in the 1983 position, Castells insists on the separation,

> while urban social movements must be connected to the political system to at least partially achieve its goals, they must be organizationally and ideologically *autonomous* of any political party. (Castells, 1983, p. 322)

The reason for this insistence on political autonomy arises from his new reading of the social system, reliant on social process, meaning here personal and group interaction, to achieve changes in value and meaning systems. Urban movements, to achieve these tasks, must be untainted by party programmes. (It should be noted that towards the end of the book, for no apparent reason, Castells uses the terms 'urban movement' and 'urban social movement' interchangeably.) Castells sees parties as bound into the 'political level', which refers in the 1983 text to the area defined in phase one as the theme of urban planning; broadly, the state apparatus operating in the interests of dominant social interests. On the other hand, urban social movements relate to a different level of the social structure, 'civil society', in which dominant values and institutional norms are not necessarily accepted. This is why urban social movements are the genuine source of social change, whereas political parties remain only at the level of political bargaining. But Castells is careful to argue that an open political system is a prerequisite for the innovations proposed by urban movements:

without an open political system, the new values, demands and desires generated by social movements not only fade (which they always do, anyway) but do not light up in the production of social reform and institutional change. (Castells, 1983, p. 294)

It is unclear in the context of this section of Castells's text whether he is referring to urban social movements or social movements in general, but his position here leads to the ambiguous conclusion that although these movements can innovate social change, they themselves cannot carry it through to a transformation of society because this depends on adaptations at the political level. Neither does this position have the possible advantage of the earlier phase of feeding urban issues into the wider political struggles, albeit through the mediation of workers' and Left parties. In place of this type of linkage Castells now argues for the cultivation of a range of key 'organizational operators'. He mentions specifically the media, professionals and political parties as the means to achieving connections to the wider society. It is not at all clear, in other words, whether in practice urban social movements can be autonomous if they are to achieve the tasks Castells, by definitional fiat, assigns them. Furthermore, the concluding discussion in *The City and the Grassroots* highlights this problem. In the last few pages, he restates his view of the significance of the urban and urban movements:

> It is precisely because the alternative projects of change in the dimensions of production, culture and power have come to a stalemate that urban social movements have been able to appear and play a major social role. (Castells, 1983, p. 326)

Castells goes on to say that it is in cities where people most intensely experience, and therefore locate explanations for, economic exploitation, cultural alienation and political oppression: 'This is the basis for the urban ideology that assigns the causality of social effects to the structure of spatial forms'. People, therefore, react against these forms of oppression in the area in which they most potently experience it, the city. So the source of urban movement activity is, on the one hand, what Castells calls 'the wild city', and on the other, because the alternative avenues of change have been blocked. The labour movement, for example, has not addressed the question of the social wage, and through its political parties has become obsessed with its own programmes and ambitions to control the state. Or the monopoly control by the mass media, with its one-way informational flows, overwhelms people's cultural horizons. In the face of these nationally and internationally sustained forces, people retreat into their own home areas and revive their own territoriality, or call for local autonomy and self-management over their communities and services.

Castells develops this theme by saying:

> an urban social movement . . . cannot, however, be a social alternative, only the symptom of a social limit, because the city it projects is not, and cannot be, connected to an alternative model of production and development, for to a democratic state adapted to the world-wide process of power. Thus urban social movements are aimed at transforming the

meaning of the city without being able to transform society. They are a reaction, not an alternative. (Castells, 1983, p. 327)

By describing urban social movements as reactive organisations Castells makes a final, startling somersault because, having raised the urban system to the forefront of his analysis, he now seems to be further away from linking urban social movements to social change than in the rest of the book, and much further away than in his previous strategies. The mechanisms of social change appear to lie completely outside the jurisdiction of urban movements. Castells says that if city administrators, financiers and the police continue to dominate, then urban social movements disintegrate. We are left with a strangely vacuous observation that,

> if the political avenues remain closed, if the new central social movements (feminism, new labour, self-management, alternative communication) do not develop in their full scope, then urban movements, reactive utopias that tried to illuminate the path they could not walk, will come again, but this time, as urban shadows eager to destroy the closed walls of their captive city. (Castells, 1983, p. 327)

Urban (social) movements are totally dependent on the success of other social movements to create the conditions in which changes of 'urban meaning' can be carried through. This, of course, echoes his earlier proposition of the dependence of urban movements on other political organisations. What has changed most fundamentally in Castells's perspective is not so much his analytical method as his own political allegiance. He has swung from support for the vanguard organisations of the workers' movement, to the Eurocommunist popular front, and now, writing from the USA, has embraced non-class 'alternative' and counter-cultural movements.

In a short, penultimate section Castells clarifies his understanding of the role played by urban movements: 'they are symptoms of our contradictions, and therefore potentially capable of superseding these contradictions'. His final image is of the new urban social movements as embryos of future societies that are being nurtured within 'local utopias' created by urban movements. If *this* is the role they play, is Castells right to attach such significance to them, to the exclusion of other avenues of analytical focus? And is his notion of the 'alternative city', as a network of self-managed, 'culturally meaningful' communities (the perfect harmonisation of his three core themes) necessarily a desirable place? If it is a utopia in the original Greek sense of the word, then it is a negative non-place. Is not the lesson of the sociology of small communities, as indicated in Chapter 3, that these places are invariably narrow and parochial, or exclusive? Black ghettos or inner-city high-rise estates are hardly visions of a new society. The crucial problem with this reading is that nowhere does Castells provide any evidence that urban movements are embryos of a future city, and he gives no clues about how autonomous urban movements might, one day, instigate urban social change.

Analysing urban social movements

In Castells's reference to the retreat of city dwellers into their local communities, as a defensive mechanism against corporate and state power, he has observed a social process that is commonplace in Britain. The notion of local control over local services, the devolution of decision-making and public participation at neighbourhood level was a familiar and widely practised trend in the 1960s and 1970s. The Association for Neighbourhood Councils, for example, has for many years advocated precisely this type of programme (Dixey, 1975). Indeed, following local government reorganisation in 1973–4, which created larger-scale local service authorities, the pressure for forms of devolution of power intensified. Many local authorities have devolved their housing and social services departments into smaller administrative units (as an institutional response), although without altering the centralised decision-making procedures.

A large number of urban social movements in Britain conform to Castells's view of centrifugal retreat into small community and neighbourhoods. The problem is, as we have seen, in relating this 'reactive' response to long-term social change. Castells, in the final pages of *The City and the Grassroots*, opts for the image of urban movements as embryos, nurturing the elements of some future society. But he appears to hold out a nihilistic prospect of continuously abortive projects unless other social forces can provide a society more receptive to their innovative life-styles and political methods. But urban social movements have been important agents of social change in the 1960s and 1970s, as much of Castells's own work indicates. There are grounds for supposing that some sort of influence will continue to be felt, albeit in different forms with possible variations in intensity of activity.

The approach of this study to the understanding of urban social movements is structured around a number of key themes, some of them derived from Castells's evolving perspective and some in critical response to his work, based on a number of consistent omissions in his material.

The core precepts of this methodology are briefly summarised below. Not all of them are equally salient at any one time or in different societies, but they do contain the key analytical fields. It should be borne in mind that the approach is intended to explore the key question of the process of mobilisation, including the whole field of action and non-action. Urban social movements represent, and are buoyed up on, a diversity of social forces and social system elements and are one expression only of these societal factors. For this reason movements may fail to materialise from potent issue bases with the social/political force expended in other forms, notably through the party political arena. The focus on the mobilisation process produces four major analytical themes.

1. *The identification and definition of social bases, which may form around residential or 'non-place' bases.* Analysis of the social structure, the consumption stakes and cross-cutting associational networks are prerequisites to understanding the emergence or non-emergence of a social movement. Issues always link to the targeted social base, which may be resistant to new organisational forms or, by the same token, may be harnessed to produce militant collective action. Systematic exploration of this arena is crucial to the analysis of urban social movement types, activity and life-cycles.

2. *The theme of local political power is central to the study of urban protest.* This includes the history and structure of the systems of

local administration, and the sub-theme of central–local relations. It includes consideration of the nature of local power, both the character of party politics, which is often elite-orientated and oligarchic, and the related issue of the 'silent' exercise of power by dominant interests. The initiation of urban social movements is frequently seen to be a response to the tactical problems of penetrating this ready-made political system. Moreover, the strategies adopted by the organisations are invariably a response to their status and stakes within local political systems. These calculations inevitably feed into the organisational structure and movement types. There is a complex interface between group autonomy and the social control potential implicit in their existence. As sensors of areas of social tension the movements may be used by the authorities to target their spending decisions, so that the analysis of urban social movement activity extends to considering the screening of social protest and the responses made by the policy-making agencies. Beyond this remains the possibility of the manipulation of some forms of urban protest into a defence of the dominant value-system.

3. *Analysis must relate specifically to the ideological structuring of the urban system.* Two ideologies are particularly prominent in the British context: the notion of local representative democracy, and those around the public/private sectoral division in the urban public services.

4. *The effect that general economic climates have on the phasing and on types of movement activity.* Although the causal links are difficult to make, it is likely to be the case that general economic tendencies exert a structuring influence on prevailing social conditions. It clearly is the case that the collapse of British manufacturing industry over the last decade has disproportionately affected the inner cities and heightened existing problems, leading to severe social tensions manifested in street riots. It is also the case that the growth of squatting in the early 1970s correlates strongly with a rise in homelessness in the context of an accelerating general trend of unemployment. Pickvance argues for a specific correlation between the economic climate and the growth or decline of different movements (Pickvance, 1983), but it is a difficult factor to isolate.

These themes provide the basis for analysing and interpreting the place of urban social movements in the urban system and draw us towards the wider issues of the fundamental processes of social change and social stability.

Urban social movements in Britain in the 1980s

In this final section, the thematic presentation is used to discuss the current phase of urban social movement activity in Britain. In line with other European countries, urban protest has been much less intense in the 1980s than in the previous two decades. Writing about the 1960s and 1970s in Britain, Dunleavy was able to suggest that urban social movements, 'have shattered the public credibility of the dominant ideology of urban economic growth embraced by city politicians, local authority planners, developers and property interests' (Dunleavy, 1980, p. 157). The less vociferous phase in the 1980s may be read partly as a 'lull', reflecting the changed economic climate in which major issues of spending and fiscal control have been temporarily resolved. This leads to a switching of resources in major areas of socialised consumption – for example, to support the subsidisation of home ownership, and the voluntary sector in housing and social welfare provision. In these circumstances demand-orientated groups have not necessarily disintegrated – as Pickvance's model suggests – but have adjusted their tactical positions. There are two related elements here: first, because of the relatively stable state of the British local government system, politically and administratively, groups have adjusted the terms of their negotiating stances to capitalise on any 'insider' connections. Their demand levels have consequently been scaled down. However, the cumulative influence of this limited activity may nevertheless remain significant. As Dearlove suggests,

> to measure success solely on the basis of a one-to-one relationship between particular campaigns and demands . . . is to ignore the significance of the cumulative, or drip, effect of all this activity. (Dearlove, 1979, p. 238)

Large numbers of action groups, tenants' associations, environmental organisations and many others remain active. As we have seen, most groups do not function solely as issue movements but simultaneously acquire wider roles (assuming they have penetrated or harnessed local social system networks). Urban social movements in Britain are more sustained than many commentators imagine, although currently their operations are low-key and built on a revised negotiating platform.

Within local political systems, two additional influences are at work. First, although the evidence is somewhat speculative on a national scale, we have observed in the South Yorkshire case studies an osmosis of activists from urban-based involvements into the party political arena. The same process has also taken a large number of activists into more broadly based social movements – the women's movement, the ecology movement and the peace movement. This is the tendency, occurring belatedly in Britain, which Evers, Ceccarelli and others noted in continental societies in the late 1970s. In Britain the suggestion of a similar flow of activists, particularly into local Labour parties, has been made by Gyford (1983). He refers to the 'new urban left', an amoeba-like' group of activists – councillors, party members, community workers, political advisers – who have entered local politics as a major forum for rekindling socialist ideas and practice. The new urban Left are not characteristically drawn from the traditional working class, but have moved into an increasingly controversial and dynamic field of politics from the community development projects of the 1970s, from the radicalised wing of some professions (notably town planning and social work), from the environmental and the women's movements, and from community action groups in general. Boddy and Fudge aruge, in similar vein, that there is evidence that the new urban Left is the source of specific changes in the composition, political perspective and policies of local Labour parties: 'Many individuals have moved into the formal political arena as councillors, party activists or committed officers' (Boddy and Fudge, 1984, p. 8). These people are the British equivalent of the key activists, drawn from the professional and middle-class social strata, identified by Castells in his phase two work. They were at the centre of the continental popular fronts that led to the municipal election victories of the Left in the mid-1970s.

The second, and closely related, influence currently at work in local politics concerns the state of central–local relations. The central–local theme is an important influence on urban movement activity and, since 1979 in Britain, it has been a major stream of political controversy. As suggested earlier in the text, this builds upon a continuous political conflict, originating in the nineteenth century, but heightened by the long-term control of major tiers of local government by the Labour Party. Political conflict in recent years has been provoked by the statutory duty imposed on local authorities to sell council houses, the imposition of spending restraints on local councils and current legislation for 'rate-capping', attacks on public transport provision, and the proposal to abolish the metropolitan counties, including the GLC. These issues have led to a groundswell of opposition, not only from Labour politicians but from Conservative peers in the House of Lords and the Conservative-controlled local authority associations. As Boddy and Fudge point out, however, the notions of 'local socialism' and those of conservative 'localist' or 'constitutional' outlook should not be confused. But currently there is a united local opposition to the centralising dictates of the Thatcher government. 'Localism' is a major and deeply ingrained local government ideology which is politically very potent.

It is in this dimension of urban politics that the main thrust of urban movement activity is currently located. Urban social movements continue to negotiate autonomously, to carry out their small-scale initiatives, and to provide welfare and support services, but it is in their links to campaigns run jointly – particularly with local Labour parties and public sector trade unions – for the defence of local government and the local control of service provision that the main thrust of activity is currently located. Many activists span the worlds of union activism, party involvement and participation in urban movements.

In some areas, notably in Greater London and South Yorkshire, conscious and systematic efforts have been made, over a number of years, to broaden local decision-making beyond the party caucuses, to include the tenants' movements, local community groups, trade unions and consumer groups. This has been done partly as a means of short-circuiting the officer level in the service departments, and partly in an effort to stage a municipal socialist alternative to what is seen as the failure of the extended periods of Labour government in the 1960s and 1970s to achieve any significant changes in the distribution of wealth, or to defend adequately the public sector.

The profile of movement activity at the present time has two main facets; first, of reduced scales of activism (and not of collapse). As suggested earlier in the book, social bases differ in their degree of receptivity to new organisational forms, so that even if movements disappear after the resolution of an issue, this does not necessarily represent the obliteration of the social force, which may surface again at a later stage. Indeed, it is arguably *more difficult* to generate a renewal of a campaign, or engage in new protest action, from an established organisation. The life-cycles of urban social movements should not be read at face value or over short durations. To do so suggests a misleading pattern of rise and sudden decline. Non-organised social forces may, in addition, be less susceptible to forms of incorporation.

Second, the strategy of building alliances with local Labour parties and public sector trade unions over the central–local clash has become an important arena of involvement for some groups. Saunders argues that these types of relationship, between industrial class-based organisations and consumption movements, are very difficult to organise and sustain. The problems arise from the 'fragmented character or urban struggles' (Saunders, 1981, p. 276) and because consumption interests can cut across traditional class solidarity. Our discussion of wealth creation through house ownership, underpinned by evidence of extensive inherited housing wealth, and the overall massive scale of 'leakage' from housing resources into other forms of consumption and investment, is perhaps the clearest example of a major cross-cutting material interest in the social system. It is not simply that individualistic solutions have become fashionable under the aegis of anti-collectivist governments, but that this ideological formula is sustained by extensive housing-created wealth. But, while agreeing with Saunders that building local alliances is inherently problematic, because of the disparate nature of the organisations concerned and the interests they represent (Saunders, 1981), social movements involved in the field of the urban public services have much in common with public sector trade unions and city Labour parties. Indeed, more recently Saunders has spoken of public sector trade unions as the possible co-ordinators of local alliances: 'they occupy a strategic position since they straddle both the division between production and consumption, and that between the national and the local' (Saunders, 1984, p. 42).

The current central–local controversies appear to support this view; but whether such alliances can be sustained is a more open question. In some local authority areas, experiments to promote local government as a form of municipal socialism, with devolved and more broadly based decision-making procedures and a collectivist philosophy, have been in operation for a number of years. Some of the problems of the long-term transformation of local political systems into a form of 'local socialism' have quickly become apparent. First, a major difficulty has been to overcome the institutionally entrenched administrative procedures of middle-tier departmental officers. Rooted in professional codes, 'expert' knowledge, and a nationally structured career and occupational community, it is not easy to persuade many officers to accept new procedures which appear to imply a dilution of their powers and a political approach with which they may have little sympathy. A response to this issue by a number of authorities has been to make sizeable resource commitments to special educational programmes; Sheffield, for example, recently allocated £30,000 to the local polytechnic for training purposes of this type. Second, as Gyford points out, a danger with the strategies of the new urban Left is that they potentially operate in a vacuum, with activists and radical councillors cut off from their electorate and the mainstream of the local authority bureaucratic process. Part of the response to this problem has been the development of locally based alliances, and there is evidence that many community action groups, tenants' associations and environmental groups welcome the opportunity for joint campaigns with local Labour parties and the local government trade unions. There *is* a shared interest between the consumers of public services, the organisations that represent them, the trade unions of the employees that work for their provision, and the councillors and party activists of the new urban Left, who themselves often straddle the spectrum from consumer to provider. It is not only in Labour-controlled local authorities where this pattern of co-operation exists. Many councils of all political persuasions are receptive to locally based initiatives at a time when national government policy towards the local level is strongly centralist.

Neither should we lose sight of the activity of a more fragmented array of social movements antipathetic to the more radical alliances. The ratepayer movement, as we saw in Chapter 5, captured support on a relatively narrow range of consumption interests, which subsequently linked into an anti-Labour, anti-public services critique. However, with the 'new Right' in the political ascendancy in national politics, the organisations representing the private market and private sector solutions have largely been eclipsed. Or, as we saw with the squatters' movement, the potential exists for radical social movements to be manipulated by media distortion and differential law enforcement, between the public and private sectors, to a focus on the inadequacies of the public sector.

In Britain in the 1980s, the pattern of urban movement activity has a number of facets. The most visible and vociferous activity occurs in the joint campaigns, reminiscent of the broad alliances spoken of by Castells in *City, Class and Power* (1978). Many organisations continue on a lower plane of activity and have opted for an emphasis on insider negotiating. There is a suggestion that with the central–local axis so sharply tilted towards central control, local politicians are more receptive to local group approaches, partly because they can point to central spending limits as the cause of problems, and partly as a mechanism for building up a fund of local support in the context of the central–local clash. As a result it may be that urban social movements are not so vulnerable to manipulation or being used as sensors of local tension points (towards which spending may need to be targeted) because the jurisdiction of spending decisions current has a very strong non-local orientation.

There are echoes of both Castells's phase two and phase three work in this situation. The alliances of local organisations in defence of the urban public services is strongly reminiscent of his 'broad Left' strategy. But across the sectoral divide there are other organisations which oppose these strategies and support increased private provision. Urban social movements in Britain are not confined only to the radical Left, but are active in local politics on the Right of the political spectrum. On their own, both sets of organisations are contained in the impact they can have on the policy process and frequently attach themselves to more broadly based bodies. But the embryo analogy used by Castells in the final pages of *The City and the Grassroots* also indicates that it is only as autonomous organisations that social movements can develop a genuinely innovatory role in social change. It may indeed be the case that their time will come. But in Britain in the mid-1980s they are locked into a party-dominated political system, as seeds of the new politics in the womb of the old politics.

References

ALTHUSSER, L. (1969) *For Marx* (London: Allen Lane).
ALTHUSSER, L. and BALIBAR, E. (1970) *Reading 'Capital'* (London: New Left Books).
BAILEY, R. (1973) *The Squatters* (Harmondsworth: Penguin).
BAKER, J. and YOUNG, M. (1971) *The Hornsey Plan* (London: Association for Neighbourhood Councils).
BALDOCK, P. (1971) 'Tenants' Voice – a Study of Council Tenants Organisation with Particular Reference to Those in the City of Sheffield', unpublished PhD thesis (University of Sheffield).
BALDOCK, P. (1982) 'The Sheffield Rent Strike of 1967–8: the Development of a Tenants' Movement', in Henderson *et al.* (1982).
BALL, M. and HARLOE, M. (1974) *Housing Policy in a Socialist Country: the Case of Poland*, Centre for Environmental Studies, Research Paper No. 8.
BARAN, P. and SWEEZY, P. (1968) *Monopoly Capital* (Harmondsworth: Penguin).
BELL, C. (1969) *Middle Class Families* (London: Routledge & Kegan Paul).
BEVAN, A. (1952) *In Place of Fear* (London: Heinemann).
BLUNKETT, D. and GREEN, G. (1983) *Building from the Bottom – the Sheffield Experience*, Fabian Tract 491 (London: Fabian Society).
BODDY, M. and FUDGE, C. (eds) (1984) *Local Socialism* (London: Macmillan).
BOWLEY, M. (1945) *Housing and the State* (London: Allen & Unwin).
BROADY, M. (1956) 'The Organisation of Coronation Street Parties', *Sociological Review*, 4.
BULPITT, J.G. (1967) *Party Politics in English Local Government* (London: Longman).
CANT, D.H. (1976) *Squatting and Private Property rights*, Town Planning Discussion Paper No. 24 (London: Bartlett School of Architecture and Planning UCL).
CARR, R. (1983) *Spain 1812–1975* (London: Oxford University Press).
CASTELLS, M. (1976) 'Theory and Ideology in Urban Sociology', in Pickvance, C.G. (ed.) *Urban Sociology: Critical Essays* (London: Tavistock).
CASTELLS, M. (1977) *The Urban Question* (London: Edward Arnold).
CASTELLS, M. (1978a) *City, Class and Power* (London: Macmillan).
CASTELLS, M. (1978b) 'Urban Social Movements and the Struggle for Democracy: the Citizens' Movement in Madrid', in *International Journal of Urban and Regional Research*, 1, pp. 133–46.

CASTELLS, M. (1983) *The City and the Grassroots* (London: Edward Arnold).

CECCARELLI, P. (1982) 'Politics, Parties and Urban Movements: Western Europe', in Fainstein, N.I. and Fainstein, S.S. (eds) *Urban Policy .Under Capitalism* (Beverly Hills, Cal.: Sage).

CHRISTALLER, W. (1933) *Central Places in Southern Germany* (translated by Baskin, C.W.) (Englewood Cliffs, NJ: Prentice-Hall, 1966).

CLEGG, T. (1983) 'Decentralization and the Transition to Democracy in Spain (1976–1983)', unpublished paper, Department of Government, London School of Economics and Political Science.

CLUTTON, A.E. (1974) 'Housing: Tenure' in Coates, B.E. (ed.) *Census Atlas of South Yorkshire*, The Department of Geography, University of Sheffield.

COATES, B.E. (1974) 'Socio-Economic Groups and Persons Seeking Work' in Coates, B.E. (ed.) *Census Atlas of South Yorkshire*, The Department of Geography, University of Sheffield.

COCHRANE, A. (1981) Introduction to Section VII, 'State Intervention', in Cochrane, A., Hamnett, C., McDowell, L. (1981).

COCHRANE, A., HAMNETT, C. and McDOWELL, L. (eds) (1981) *City, Economy and Society: A Comparative Reader* (London: Harper & Row, in association with The Open University Press).

COLLISON, P. (1963) *The Cutteslowe Walls* (London: Faber & Faber).

CORBYN, P. (1980) 'We Won, You Should Fight Them Too', in Wates, N. and Wolmar, C. (eds).

CREWE, I. (1979) 'Who Swung Tory?', in *The Economist*, 12 May.

DARKE, R. (1983) Review of Friedland, R. (1982) in *Housing and Planning Review*, Vol. 38, No. 2, p. 24.

DEAR, M. and SCOTT, A.J. (eds) (1981) *Urbanization and Urban Planning in Capitalist Society* (London: Methuen).

DEARLOVE, J. (1973) *The Politics of Policy in Local Government* (Cambridge: Cambridge University Press).

DEARLOVE, J. (1979) *The Reorganisation of British Local Government* (Cambridge: Cambridge University Press).

DENNIS, N. *et al.* (1957) *Coal is our Life* (London: Eyre & Spottiswoode).

DIXEY, R. (1975) *A Guide to Neighbourhood Councils* (Association for Neighbourhood Councils).

DUNLEAVY, P. (1977) 'Protest and Quiescence in Urban Politics: a Critique of Some Pluralist and Structuralist Myths', *International Journal of Urban and Regional Research*, 1, pp. 193–218.

DUNLEAVY, P. (1979) 'Some Political Implications of Sectoral Cleavages and the Growth of State Employment', in *Political Studies*, 27.

DUNLEAVY, P. (1980) *Urban Political Analysis* (London: Macmillan).

DUNLEAVY, P. (1983) 'Socialized Consumption and Economic Development', draft paper to Anglo-Dutch Seminar on Local State Research, University of Copenhagen.

DURANT, R. (now Glass) (1939) *Watling: A Survey of Social Life on a New Housing Estate* (London: P.S. King)

EVERS, A. (1981) 'Social Movements and Political Power: A Survey of a Theoretical and Political Controversy', in *Comparative Urban Research*, February.

FAINSTEIN, N.I. and FAINSTEIN, S.S. (eds) (1982) *Urban Policy Under Capitalism* (Beverly Hills: Sage).

FORREST, R. and MURIE, A. (1984) *Right to Buy? Issues of Need, Equity and Polarisation in the Sale of Council Houses*, Working Paper No. 39 (Bristol: University of Bristol, School for Advanced Urban Studies).

FRANKENBERG, R. (1966) *Communities in Britain* (Harmondsworth: Penguin).

FRIEDLAND, R. (1982) *Power and Crisis in the City* (London: Macmillan).

FRIEND, A. (1980) 'The Post War Squatters', in Wates, N. and Wolmar, C. (eds).

GEORGE, V. and WILDING, P. (1976) *Ideology and Social Welfare* (London: Routledge & Kegan Paul).

GIMSON, M. (1980) 'Everybody's Doing it: a Look at Some of the World's Diverse Squatting Movements', in Wates, N. and Wolmar, C. (eds).

GOETSCHIUS, G.W. (1969) *Working with Community Groups* (London: Routledge & Kegan Paul).

GOLDSMITH, M. (1982) *Politics, Planning and the City* (London: Hutchinson).

GRANT, W. (1977) *Independent Local Politics in England and Wales* (Farnborough: Saxon House).

GRAY, F. (1979) 'Consumption: Council House Management', Chapter 8 in Merrett, S. *State Housing in Britain* (London: Routledge & Kegan Paul).

GREEN, D.G. (1981) *Power and Party in an English City* (London: Allen & Unwin).

GYFORD, J. (1983) 'The New Urban Left: a Local Road to Socialism?', in *New Society*, 21 April.

HADDON, R. (1970) 'A Minority in a Welfare State Society', in *New Atlantis*, Vol. 2.

HAMPTON, W.A. (1968) 'The Electoral Response to a Multi-Vote Ballot', in *Political Studies*, Vol. XVI, No. 2.

HAMPTON, W.A. (1970) *Democracy and Community* (London: Oxford University Press).

HARLOE, M. (ed.) (1977) *Captive Cities: Studies in the Political Economy of Cities and Regions* (London: Wiley).

HARLOE, M. (1981) 'Notes on Comparative Urban Research', in Dear, M. and Scott, A.J. (1981).

HARLOE, M. (1984) 'Sector and Class: a Critical Comment', in *International Journal of Urban and Regional Research*, 8.

HAWLEY, A.H. (1950) *Human Ecology: A Theory of Community Structure* (New York: Wiley).

HENDERSON, P., WRIGHT, A. and WYNOLL, K. (eds) (1982) *Successes and Struggles on Council Estates: Tenant Action and Community Work* (London: Association of Community Workers).

HODGES, A.W. and SMITH, C.S. (1954) 'The Sheffield Estate', in *Neighbourhood and Community* (Liverpool: Liverpool University Press).

IWANICKA-LYRA, E. (1972) 'Changes in the Character of Migration Movements from Rural to Urban Areas in Poland', reprinted in Cochrane, A., Hamnett, C., McDowell, L. (eds) (1981).

JACKSON, B. (1968) *Working Class Community* (London: Routledge & Kegan Paul).

JANOWITZ, M. (1952) *The Community Press in an Urban Setting* (Chicago: Chicago University Press).

JANSSEN, R. (1978) 'Class Practices of Dwellers in Barrios Populares: the Struggle for the Right to the City', in *International Journal of Urban and Regional Research*, 1, pp. 147–59.

KATZNELSON, I. (1981) *City Trenches: Urban Politics and the Patterning of Class in the United States* (New York: Pantheon).

KATZNELSON, I., GILLE, K. and WEIR, M. (1982) 'Race and Schooling: Reflections on the Social Bases of Urban Movements', in Fainstein, N.I. and Fainstein, S.S. (eds) (1982).

KEMENY, J. (1980) 'Home Ownership and Privatisation', in *International Journal of Urban and Regional Research*, Vol. 4.

KEMENY, J. and THOMAS, A. (1984) 'Capital Leakage from Owner-Occupied Housing', in *Policy and Politics*, Vol. 12, No. 1.

KENEDI, J. (undated) *Do It Yourself: Hungary's Hidden Economy* (London: Pluto).

KING, R. and NUGENT, N. (1978) 'Ratepayers Associations in Newcastle and Wakefield', in Garrard, J. *et al.* (eds) *The Middle Class in Politics* (Farnborough: Saxon House).

LAMBERT, J., PARIS, C., and BLACKABY, B. (1978) *Housing Policy and the State* (London: Macmillan).

LÖSCH, A. (1939) *The Economics of Location* (New Haven: Yale University Press, 1954).

LOWE, S.G. (1977) 'Local Politics and Community Groups', in Darke, R. and Walker, R. (eds) *Local Government and the Public* (London: Leonard Hill).

LOWE, S.G. (1980) 'Local Politics and Community Groups', unpublished PhD thesis (University of Sheffield).

LOWE, S.G. (1985) 'Wealth, Inheritance and Home Ownership' (forthcoming).

LUKES, S. (1975) *Power: a Radical View* (London: Macmillan).

LUPTON, T. and MITCHELL, D. (1954) 'The Liverpool Estate', in *Neighbourhood and Community* (Liverpool: Liverpool University Press).

MALPASS, P. and MURIE, A. (1982) *Housing Policy and Practice* (London: Macmillan).

MARCELLONI, M. (1979) 'Urban Movements and Political Struggles in Italy', in *International Journal of Urban and Regional Research*, Vol. 3.

MELLING, J. (1979) 'The Glasgow Rent Strike and Clydeside Labour: Some Problems of Interpretation', in *Journal of the Scottish Labour History Society*, 13.

MELLING, J. (1980) 'Clydeside Housing and the Evolution of State Rent Control, 1900–1939' in Melling, J. (ed.) *Housing, Social Policy and the State* (London: Croom Helm).

MIDDLEMAS, R.K. (1964) *The Clydesiders* (London: Hutchinson).

MISHAN, E.J. (1967) *The Costs of Economic Growth* (Harmondsworth: Penguin).

MOORHOUSE, B., WILSON, M. and CHAMBERLAIN, C. (1972) 'Rent Strikes – Direct Action and the Working Class', in *The Socialist Register, 1972* (London: Merlin).

MORRIS, R.N. and MOGEY, J.F. (1954) 'The Sheffield Estate', in *Neighbourhood and Community* (Liverpool: Liverpool University Press).

MURIE, A. and FORREST, R. (198?) 'Wealth, Inheritance and Housing Policy', in *Policy and Politics*, Vol. 8, No. 1.

MURIE, A. and FORREST, R. (1984) *Right to Buy? Issues of Need, Equity and Polarisation in the Sale of Council Houses*, Working Paper 39 (Bristol: University of Bristol School for Advanced Urban Studies).

MUSGRAVE, S. (1984) 'Housing in Czechoslovakia', in *Housing Review*, Vol. 33, No. 3.

NEWTON, K. (1976) *Second City Politics* (London: Oxford University Press).

NUGENT, N. (1979) 'The Ratepayers', in Ring, R. and Nugent, N. (eds) *Respectable Rebels* (London: Hodder & Stoughton).

OLIVES, J. (1976) 'The Struggle against Urban Renewal in the "Cite de Alliarte" ' in Pickvance, C.G. (ed.) *Urban Sociology: Critical Essays* (London: Tavistock).

PAHL, R.E. (1968) 'Class and Community in an English Commuter Village', in Pahl, R.E. (ed.) *Readings in Urban Sociology* (Oxford: Pergamon).

PAHL, R.E. (1970) *Patterns of Urban Life* (London: Longman).

PAHL, R.E. (1975) 'Urban Managerialism Reconsidered', in Pahl, R.E. (ed.) *Whose City?*, second edn (London: Longman).

PARIS, C. and POPPLESTON, G. (1978) *Squatting: a Bibliography*, Occasional Paper No. 3 (Birmingham: Centre for Environmental Studies).

PARK, R.E. (1929) *Human Communities* (New York: Free Press, 1952).

PARK, R.E., BURGESS, E.W. and McKENZIE, R.D. (1925) *The City* (Chicago: Chicago University Press).

PARKIN, F. (1971) *Class Inequality and Political Order* (London: MacGibbon & Kee).

PICKVANCE, C.G. (1976a) 'On the Study of Urban Social Movements', in Pickvance (ed.) (1976).

PICKVANCE, C.G. (ed.) (1976a) *Urban Sociology: Critical Essays* (London: Tavistock).

PICKVANCE, C.G. (1982) *The State and Collective Consumption*, Unit 24 of Open University course D202 *Urban Change and Conflict* (Milton Keynes: The Open University Press).

PICKVANCE, C.G. (1983) 'What Has Become of Urban Movements? Towards a Comparative Analysis of a Diverse Reality', paper for the Conference on 'La mise en question de l'état-providence et émergence de la cité', University of Paris X, Nanterre.

PIEKALKIEWICZ, J. (1975) 'Polish Local Government: Conflicts of Interest Within the Monolith', reprinted in Cochrane, A., Hamnett, C. and McDowell, L. (eds) (1981).

PIVEN, F.F. and CLOWARD, R.A. (1977) *Poor People's Movements: Why they Succeed, How they Fail* (New York: Pantheon).

PLATT, S. (1980) 'Setting the Stage', in Wates, N. and Wolmar, C. (eds).

POULANTZAS, N. (1973) *Political Power and Social Class* (London: New Left Books).

REX, J. and MOORE, R. (1967) *Race, Community and Conflict* (London: Oxford University Press).

REX, J. (1973) *Race, Colonialism and the City* (London: Routledge & Kegan Paul).

RICHARDS, P.G. (1967) 'Southampton', in Sharpe, L.J. (ed.) *Voting in Cities* (London: Macmillan).

RUNCIMAN, W. (1966) *Relative Deprivation and Social Justice* (London: Routledge & Kegan Paul).

SAUNDERS, P. (1979) *Urban Politics: A Sociological Approach* (London: Hutchinson).

SAUNDERS, P. (1981) *Social Theory and the Urban Question* (London: Hutchinson).

SAUNDERS, P. (1982) *Beyond Housing Classes: The Sociological Significance of Private Property Rights in Means of Consumption*, Working Paper 33, Urban and Regional Studies, University of Sussex.

SAUNDERS, P. (1984) 'Rethinking Local Politics', in Boddy, M. and Fudge, C. (eds).

SELF-HELP HOUSING RESOURCE LIBRARY (1980) 'Bibliography', in Wates, N. and Wolmar, C. (eds).

SERAFIN, R. (1982) 'The Greening of Poland', in *The Ecologist*, Vol. 12, No. 4.

SHARPE, L.J. (ed.) (1967) *Voting in Cities* (London: Macmillan).

SHARPE, L.J. (1979) *Decentralist Trends in Western Europe* (London: Sage).

SHEFSKY, E. and BELL, W. (1955) *Social Area Analysis* (Stanford: Stanford University Press).

SKLAIR, L. (1975) 'The Struggle Against the Housing Finance Act', in *The Socialist Register, 1975* (London: Merlin).

SPILERMAN, S. (1970) 'The Causes of Racial Disturbances: a Comparison of Alternative Explanations', *American Sociological Review*, 35.

SPILERMAN, S. (1971) 'The Causes of Racial Disturbances: Tests of an Explanation', *American Sociological Review*, 36.

SPILERMAN, S. (1974) 'Structural Characteristics of Cities and the Severity of Racial Disorders', Institute for Research on Poverty, discussion papers, Madison, Wisconsin.

STANYER, J. (1967) 'Exeter', in Sharpe, L.J. (ed.) *Voting in Cities* (London: Macmillan).

SUTTLES, G.D. (1972) *The Social Construction of Communities* (Chicago: Chicago University Press).

WATES, N. and WOLMAR, C. (eds) (1980) *Squatting: The Real Story* (London: Bay Leaf Books).

WATKINSON, D. and REED, M. (1976) *Squatting and Civil Liberties* (London: National Council for Civil Liberties).

WAUGH, S. (1976) *Needs and Provision for Young Single Homeless People* (London: CHAR).

WESTERGAARD, J. (1965) 'The Withering Away of Class', in Anderson, P. and Blackburn, R. (eds) *Towards Socialism* (London: Fontana).

WILMOTT, P. and YOUNG, M. (1970) *Family and Class in a London Suburb* (London: Routledge & Kegan Paul).

WIRTH, L. (1928) *The Ghetto* (Chicago: Chicago University Press).

WIRTH, L. (1938) 'Urbanism as a Way of Life', *American Journal of Sociology*, Vol. 44, pp. 1–24.

WOLMAR, C. (1981) 'The Tenants' Movement', in *Roof*, November/December.

WOOD, T. (1980) 'Is There Life After Squatting?' in Wates, N. and Wolmar, C. (eds).

Index